Crusaders
IN THE
Holy Land

■ ■ ■ ■ ■ ■ ■ ■

THE ARCHAEOLOGY OF FAITH

*A collection of essays published
by the Biblical Archaeology Society*

CONTRIBUTORS

DAN BAHAT
JACK MEINHARDT
YAAKOV MESHORER
ROBERT OUSTERHOU
BARGIL PIXNER
ERIC WARGO
WARREN T. WOODFIN
WALTER ZANGER

D1532479

EDITOR
JACK MEINHARDT

◉ BIBLICAL ARCHAEOLOGY SOCIETY

On the cover:
Mounted bishops lead the Crusaders into the Holy Land, in this illustration from the anonymous medieval Provençal work, *Universal History: From the Creation of the World to the Death of Emperor Henry the Seventh*. Composed in the early 14th-century, the manuscript is now in the British Library.
Photo ©British Library/HIP/Art Resource, NY.

Library of Congress Cataloging-in-Publication Data
Crusaders in the Holy Land: the archaeology of faith: a collection of essays published by
the Biblical Archaeology Society
contributors: Jack Meinhardt ... [et al.]; editor: Jack Meinhardt
p. cm.
ISBN 1-880317-80-X
1. Jerusalem (Latin Kingdom) 2. Crusades 3. Palestine—History—750-1260 4. Jerusalem—Antiquities
I. Meinhardt, Jack, 1956- II. Biblical Archaeology Society
D178.C78 2005
956.94'032—dc22   2005015917

©2005 Biblical Archaeology Society
4710 41st St., NW
Washington, DC 20016

All rights reserved under Pan-American Copyright Conventions.
Printed in the United States of America.
Design by Auras Design.

C O N T E N T S

✠

CONTRIBUTORS

Dan Bahat, one of the world's foremost experts on the Crusader period in the Holy Land, is a senior lecturer at Bar-Ilan University. He has served as district archaeologist for both Jerusalem and the Galilee, and as a consulting archaeologist for excavations at the Temple Mount wall. Bahat has directed digs at Tel Dan, the Beth-Shean synagogue and Herod's Palace in Jerusalem. In 1989 he became only the third person to receive the Jerusalem Award for Archaeology.

Yaakov Meshorer, until his death in 2004, was curator of the Department of Numismatics at the Israel Museum and a professor at Hebrew University in Jerusalem. He wrote widely throughout his life on ancient Jewish coinage and inscriptions.

Robert Ousterhout is chair of the department of architectural history and preservation at the University of Illinois. He has directed a survey of Byzantine settlements in Cappadocia, central Turkey. His books include *Master Builders of Byzantium* (Princeton University Press, 1999) and *The Art of Kariye Camii* (Scala Publishers, 2002). Recently he was awarded a grant for the restoration of the Zeyrek Camii in Istanbul.

Bargil Pixner, who died in 2002, was an archaeologist and Benedictine monk. Father Pixner lived in the Dormition Abbey on Mount Zion and taught biblical archaeology to students and pilgrims. He is the author of *With Jesus in Jerusalem: His First and Last Days in Judea* (Corazin Publishing, 1996).

Eric Wargo, former associate editor of *Bible Review* magazine, is currently a freelance writer and a managing editor with the American Psychological Society. He has published a number of articles on medieval symbolism.

Warren T. Woodfin, a postdoctoral research fellow at Princeton University, is completing a book on Byzantine liturgical vestments and their embroidered decoration. His research focuses on the intersections between ecclesial liturgies and the ceremonies of statecraft in Byzantium and the medieval West. Prior to his research at Princeton, he served as a Junior Fellow at Dumbarton Oaks and a visiting assistant professor in Art and Art History at Duke University.

Walter Zanger, one of Israel's best-known tour guides, appears regularly as a commentator on television and radio and has written a number of documentary films. He has worked for the *Jerusalem Post* and contributed to the *Encyclopedia Judaica*. He is also an ordained rabbi.

LIST OF ILLUSTRATIONS

PREFACE

This slim book, consisting of articles from *Biblical Archaeology Review, Bible Review* and *Archaeology Odyssey*, does not pretend to be comprehensive or exhaustive. It simply offers a glimpse of one of the most fascinating, puzzling, brilliant and tortured episodes in Western history—a time when men and women refused to take their faith for granted and acted on what they believed were the commands of God, often with devastating effects. It was a time when West met East, when pious monks became fierce soldiers, when kings felt compelled to abandon the luxury of their palaces and "take the cross." The authors in this volume are generally interested in what the Crusaders left behind in the Holy Land, the material remains of that most curious period of colonization. Although the Crusaders built palaces and castle-fortresses (some breathtakingly beautiful in their desolate settings), their principal achievement was their churches, the palpable testament of their faith. That is why the subtitle of this book is "The Archaeology of Faith," even though faith cannot be revealed with a spade.

Jack Meinhardt
Editor

CHAPTER 1

When Crusader Kings Ruled Jerusalem

JACK MEINHARDT

It was one of the most romantic, chaotic, cruel, passionate, bizarre and dramatic episodes in history. In the 12th and 13th centuries A.D., a continual stream of European armies, mustered mostly in present-day France and Germany, marched out to destroy the infidel. Crusaders attacked non-Christians in northern and eastern Europe; they conducted bloody pogroms against Jews and "heretical" Christians in their own territories; they campaigned to push Muslims off the Iberian peninsula and out of North Africa; and, most important of all, they conquered Palestine, ruling the Holy Land from their citadel in Jerusalem.

Easily the most successful of these campaigns was the First Crusade (1096–1099). Palestine had been in Muslim hands since the seventh century, when Persians and then Arabs wrested it from the Christian Byzantine Empire. In the mid-11th century, Seljuk Turks from beyond the Caspian Sea invaded the Near East, converted to Islam and subdued the reigning Arab power, the Abbasid caliphate in Baghdad. They then pressed north and west, seizing most of Byzantine Anatolia. The Seljuk advance meant that Christian influence in the East was considerably diminished. It also meant that pilgrimage routes, long protected by the Byzantines and friendly Arab rulers, were closed down: Christians could no longer walk where Jesus had walked.

The Byzantine emperor Alexius I appealed to the West for help. In 1095 Pope Urban II responded; in a speech delivered at Cler-

Crusader Palestine

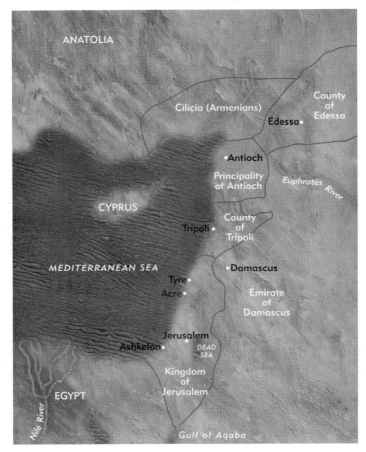

mont, in central France, he called for a crusade to save the Christian East from Islam. Seljuk Turks, Urban reportedly said, were disemboweling Christians and dumping the bloody viscera on church altars and baptismal fonts. Those who joined this crusade and "took the cross," the pope announced, would have their sins absolved, for God himself desired that Christianity recover Jerusalem.

The First Crusade, like most of the later ones, was led by European noble and royal families, who raised funds and armies from their estates. (Even the official, pope-sponsored crusades, however, were joined by ragtag groups of women, children, paupers, priests and elderly penitents.) One army, for example, was led by three brothers with possessions in Lorraine, Eustace, Godfrey and Baldwin; Godfrey and Baldwin would become the first rulers of the Latin Kingdom of Jerusalem. Other Crusaders were the king of France's brother, Hugh of Vermandois, and William the Conqueror's son, Robert of Normandy. A Norman family that had settled in southern Italy sent Tancred, who was the first to lead Crusader troops into Jerusalem and onto the Temple Mount.

These armies marched overland to Constantinople, where Emperor Alexius I ferried them across the Bosphorus into Asia. They then crossed Anatolia and laid siege to Antioch, which fell in 1098—becoming the first Crusader colony in the Near East.

Most of the Crusader forces continued south, facing little resistance as they moved down the Levantine coast. On July 15, 1099, after a two-week siege of Jerusalem, Tancred broke through the city's northern wall, near Herod's Gate. The city's Muslim rulers surrendered without a fight. The next morning, however, Jerusalem became a killing field as the conquerors slaughtered nearly every Muslim in the city and burned down a synagogue in which Jews had sought refuge. "With drawn swords our men ran through the city not sparing anyone, even those begging for mercy," wrote Fulcher of Chartres, who served as Baldwin's chaplain. "They desired that this place, so long contaminated by the superstition of the pagan inhabitants, should be cleansed from their contagion."

The Crusaders elected Godfrey as their first leader. Upon Godfrey's death in 1100, they named his brother Baldwin as the first official king of the Latin Kingdom of Jerusalem (which, in its brief tenure, would have four more kings named Baldwin). In the following decades, the new Crusader kingdom secured the main coastal cities of the Levant: Caesarea (1101), Haifa and Acre (1104), Beirut and Sidon (1110), and Tyre (1124). King Baldwin I (1100–1118) took territories in the Transjordan and built a series of fortresses from the Dead Sea to the Gulf of Aqaba. King Baldwin III (1152–1163) captured Ashkelon from the Egyptian Fatimid dynasty, which was using the city's port to conduct raids against the Crusader kingdom. By the mid-12th century, the Latin Kingdom of Jerusalem controlled the territories of present-day Israel, western Jordan and southern Lebanon. In addition, the Crusaders had set up states in Edessa, Antioch and Tripoli. The entire Levant was now a European colony.

On the holy city of Jerusalem itself, the Crusaders left little mark. At first, their activities were concentrated on the Temple Mount. From indigenous Near Eastern Christians, the Crusaders learned that the Temple Mount was associated with such biblical events as the presentation of Christ in the Temple (Luke 2:22–38) and Jacob's dream of a ladder to heaven (Genesis 28:11–17). The Crusaders immediately converted the Muslim Dome of the Rock—which, they were told, rested on the site of the Jewish Temple mentioned in the Gospels—into a Christian church, which they called the Templum Domini. They later covered the massive rock inside the building with elaborate marble casing, to serve as an altar; they also filled the building's niches with sacred carvings, erected an intricate iron grille around the building's inner octagon, and placed an iron cross on top of the dome.

Crusader kings first took up residence in the Al-Aqsa Mosque, on the southern end of the Temple Mount; but in 1118 they abandoned the mosque for the newly rebuilt citadel, south of the Tower of David. Al-Aqsa then became the residence of the Templar Knights—an order first created to protect pilgrim routes and later transformed into an elite fighting force. Outside the Temple Mount, the Crusaders built a covered market, a new city gate (Tanners' Gate), a hospital (run by the Knights of the Order of St. John, also known as the Hospitallers, who, like the Templars, were first founded to care for pilgrims but later became a military force) and various other buildings.

What the Crusaders really built, however, were churches, a number of which still survive in excellent condition. East of the city, on the Mount of Olives, they built the Church of the Tomb of the Virgin over an earlier Byzantine structure, which, according to tradition, contained the tomb of Mary. In this church the Crusaders placed the tomb of Queen Melisende (1131–1152), the daughter of Baldwin II. Just north of the northeast corner of the Temple Mount, they erected the splendid Romanesque Church of St. Anne.

Crusader Jerusalem

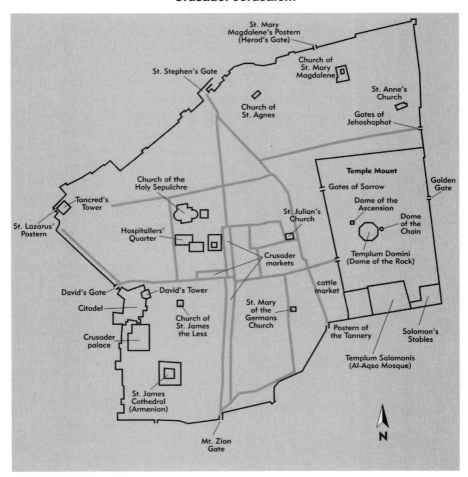

The Crusaders' most enduring architectural legacy, however, was their rebuilding of the Church of the Holy Sepulchre on the foundations of the fourth-century A.D. church built by Constantine, supposedly over Jesus' tomb.

Crusader rule in Jerusalem lasted a mere 90 years. In 1187 the sultan Saladin, who had unified Egyptian and Syrian territories into the Abbasid caliphate, defeated the army of the Latin Kingdom of Jerusalem at the Horns of Hattin, west of the Sea of

Galilee, and took control of Jerusalem. For two brief periods in the 13th century, between 1229 and 1244, Crusaders regained control of Jerusalem—but only by treaty with the Muslim Ayyubids (a new caliphate formed by Saladin's successors), who refused to allow Christians to visit the sacred Temple Mount.

After Saladin's conquest, the Latin kings ruled their diminished territory from the coastal cities of Tyre and Acre (Akko), not from Jerusalem. Their holdings consisted of a thin strip along the Mediterranean, which expanded during Crusades (altogether there were seven official crusades in the 12th and 13th centuries, along with countless smaller ones) and contracted as the Crusaders returned home.

In the late 13th century, a new force arose in Egypt, the Mamluks, a class of fierce slave warriors who wrested power from the Ayyubids. The Mamluk sultan Baybars campaigned up the Levantine coast, regaining Crusader possessions. The last Crusader outpost, the city of Acre, fell in 1291, putting an end to the European presence in Palestine.

The Holiest Ground in the World

How the Crusaders Transformed Jerusalem's Temple Mount

WARREN T. WOODFIN

After defeating the army of the Latin Kingdom of Jerusalem at the Horns of Hattin, west of the sea of Galilee, in 1187, the Egyptian sultan Saladin marched unopposed into Jerusalem. European Crusaders, mostly from the region of present-day France, had occupied the ancient city for almost a century, following 450 years of Arab rule. Saladin's reclamation of one of Islam's holiest sites, the Dome of the Rock on Jerusalem's Temple Mount, spurred the Arab historian Imad ad-Din to impressive heights of rhetoric:

> The Rock, the object of pilgrimage, was hidden under constructions and submerged in all this sumptuous building. So the Sultan ordered that the veil should be removed, the curtain raised, the concealments taken away, the marble carried off, the stones broken, the structures demolished, the covers broken into. The Rock was to be brought to light again for visitors and revealed to observers, stripped of its covering and brought forward like a young bride. He wanted the pearl extracted from its shell, the full moon brought from behind the clouds, the prison torn down, the condemned ransomed, its beauty revealed, its blessed aspect allowed to shine, its true face made clear, its genuine honour brought to light, its fine state restored, its high honour and standing brought back. Surely it is something

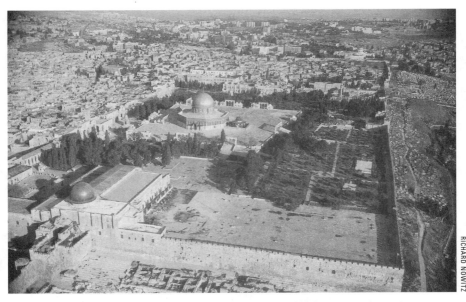

The Temple Mount—a nearly rectangular platform 1,600 feet long on its eastern (right) side and 920 feet wide on its southern (bottom) side—was originally
built by the Jewish king Herod the Great (37-4 B.C.) to support the Jerusalem
Temple. In the late seventh century A.D., the Islamic Umayyad caliphate, cen-
tered in Damascus, built the Dome of the Rock and the Al-Aqsa Mosque on the
Temple Mount, which they called the Haram al-Sharif, or Noble Sanctuary.

whose beauty consists in being unadorned, whose nakedness is clothing and whose clothing is nakedness. It was
restored to its former state and the outstanding splendor
of its beauty was brought into the open.[1]

Saladin's men cleared away the Crusader additions to the Dome
of the Rock. Then the Temple Mount, called the Haram al-Sharif
(Noble Sanctuary) by the Arabs, was purified with incense and
rose water.[2]

This purging of reminders of Christian occupation complicates
the task of understanding the works carried out by the Crusaders
on the Temple Mount. Most of the Crusader remains are architectural fragments in secondary use, often with such offending
elements as crosses and human faces chiseled off. However, we
do have accounts by Crusaders, pilgrims and resident Arabs that

provide a glimpse of 12th-century architectural activity on the Haram. From these accounts and the scant archaeological remains, we can see how medieval Europeans, armed with the holy scriptures and inspired by legends of apostles, saints and martyrs, confronted the physical fabric of an earthly Jerusalem.

The Crusaders found a city little changed by the centuries of Muslim domination. Jerusalem's Muslim rulers had constructed their most important buildings on the Haram al-Sharif, a site that was (and remains today) extremely important in three of the world's major religions: Judaism, Christianity and Islam. In Jewish tradition this was Mt. Moriah, where Abraham prepared to sacrifice his son Isaac; similarly, in Islamic tradition the Haram was the site where Abraham prepared to sacrifice his son Ishmael. According to the Hebrew Bible, it was here that King Solomon built the First Temple to house the Ark of the Covenant, which was made by the early Israelites to contain the tablets inscribed with the Ten Commandments. In the late first century B.C., the Judean king Herod the Great vastly expanded the site (to its present-day proportions) by constructing a huge platform to support the Second Temple, which was destroyed by the Romans in 70 A.D.

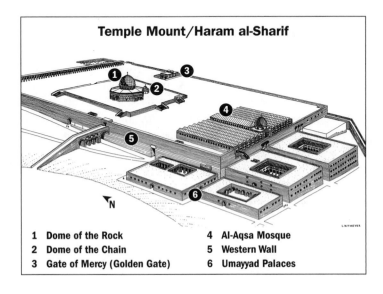

Temple Mount/Haram al-Sharif

1	Dome of the Rock	4 Al-Aqsa Mosque
2	Dome of the Chain	5 Western Wall
3	Gate of Mercy (Golden Gate)	6 Umayyad Palaces

For the next 600 years, during Roman (70–326) and Byzantine (326–638) rule, the Temple Mount was largely ignored. Things changed again in the seventh century, when Arab Muslims captured Jerusalem and reconverted the Haram into a holy sanctuary, this time of Islam. At its center, the Umayyad caliph Abd al-Malik (685–705) built the glimmering, octagonal Dome of the Rock over es-Sakhra—a rock outcropping where, according to early Muslim tradition, King David had prayed to God and King Solomon had built the Temple. (Later Muslim tradition identified es-Sakhra as the place from which the prophet Mohammed [c. 570–632] ascended to heaven after his night journey from Mecca.)[3] In the early eighth century, the Umayyads built the large silver-domed Al-Aqsa Mosque on the Haram's southern end. For Muslims, as for Jews and later for the Crusaders, the Haram/Temple Mount was closely associated with the presence of God.

When the Crusaders stormed Jerusalem on July 15, 1099, one of the world's holiest sites became a slaughterhouse. After the Crusaders led by Tancred breached Jerusalem's northern gate and gained the Haram, the Muslims fled to the al-Aqsa Mosque, where they surrendered to the Crusaders. The next morning, however, the Crusaders entered the mosque, slaughtered the Muslim prisoners and then moved on to kill thousands of Muslims and a number of Jews throughout Jerusalem. One observer recalled: "In the Temple and porch of Solomon, men rode in blood up to their knees and bridle reins."[4]

Amid the heaped-up corpses on the Haram, the Crusaders found three major Islamic buildings: the Dome of the Rock, standing on its own platform near the center of the mount, surrounded by shimmering arcades; the smaller Dome of the Chain, east of the Dome of the Rock; and the Al-Aqsa Mosque, at the southern edge of the mount. Numerous gates led to the sacred precinct, though the most monumental of them, the Golden Gate, traditionally the gate through which Jesus entered Jerusalem riding on a donkey, was most likely blocked at the time.[5] Built into the southeast corner of the mount was a small underground mosque, which supposedly contained relics of Jesus' infancy—the bed of the Virgin, as well as the crib and bath of the infant.[6]

The Crusaders considered the Haram a sacred place, even

ISRAEL MINISTRY OF TOURISM

According to tradition, the Dome of the Rock rests on ground sacred to Jews, Christians and Muslims. Here Abraham prepared to sacrifice his son Isaac (for Jews and Christians) or Ishmael (for Muslims); here Solomon built his Temple to the Lord; here the young Jesus was presented to the Temple as the Messiah; and here Mohammed ascended to heaven.

though the great platform had been built by a Jewish king, Herod the Great, and all its structures had been built by Muslims. Almost from the beginning of Christian rule over Jerusalem, Crusader texts and maps refer to the Dome of the Rock as the Templum Domini (Temple of the Lord) and to the Al-Aqsa Mosque as the Templum Salomonis (Temple of Solomon). This is in remarkable contrast to the earlier period of Byzantine rule, when the Christians left the Temple Mount in neglect. Why the sudden interest? Were the Crusaders, deluded by their passionate quest to reclaim holy ground, simply ignorant of the Haram/Temple Mount's history?

During the periods of Byzantine and Arab rule, Jerusalem had been a destination for Christian pilgrims from the West. (Pilgrimage routes were kept open until the mid-11th century, when the Seljuk Turks took control of the Levant and closed them down.) In some accounts, pilgrims associate the Haram with Solomon's Temple and describe its contemporaneous structures as having

ISRAEL MINISTRY OF TOURISM

The Church of the Holy Sepulchre was first built by the emperor Constantine (306-337 A.D.), supposedly over the tomb of Jesus. The Crusaders found the church in ruins, so they built a much larger cathedral (dedicated in 1142) on the earlier foundations. This photo shows the Crusader church's main facade. From Europe the Crusaders brought Romanesque architecture, especially prominent in the church's vaults, moderately pointed arches, cupolas and ornamented capitals.

been built by Muslims.[7] As a rule, however, Byzantine Christians and early Western pilgrims showed little interest in the site: If the Haram was indeed the site of the Jerusalem Temple, then, according to the Gospels, God himself had chosen to destroy it. Did not Jesus prophesy: "I will destroy this temple that is made with hands, and in three days I will build another, not made with hands" (Mark 14:58)? For early Christians, another site in Jerusalem had superseded the Temple Mount as the holiest of grounds: the Church of the Holy Sepulchre, which was built—supposedly over Jesus' tomb—by the emperor Constantine (306–337 A.D.).

Once the Crusaders took control of Jerusalem, however, they began to reinterpret the significance of the Haram. A Russian pilgrim who visited Jerusalem in the early 12th century refers to the Dome of the Rock interchangeably as the "Mosque of Omar" and the "Church of the Holy of Holies."[8] Some Western pilgrims during the Crusader period seem to have believed that they were seeing the very Temple built by Solomon.[9] Even writers somewhat familiar with the history of the site differ greatly over who built the Dome of the Rock. One anonymous Latin source, for example, records the several destructions of the Temple of Jerusalem— by the Babylonian king Nebuchadnezzar (in 586 B.C.), by the Seleucid king Antiochus (281–261 B.C.) and by the Roman general Titus (70 A.D.)—and then goes on to speculate about the possible builders of the extant temple: Emperor Constantine (306–337) and his mother, Helena; Emperor Justinian (527–565) or Emperor Heraclius (610–641); or an Egyptian prince.[10]

By the time the Crusaders arrived in Jerusalem, it appears, Christians no longer cared who built the Dome of the Rock, or when it was done. What mattered was that the Temple—whether the work of Jews, Christians or Muslims—sat on a holy site sanctified by the Bible, as one Crusader wrote:

> To the east, below Mt. Calvary, is the Temple of the Lord [the Dome of the Rock], in another part of the city, which was built by Solomon ... In the middle of the Temple is a great mount [es-Sakhra] surrounded by walls, in which is the Tabernacle; there also was the Ark of the Covenant which, after the destruction of the Temple, was taken away to Rome by the Emperor Vespasian.[11]

The earliest Crusader accounts indicate that the contents of the biblical Tabernacle would soon be found within the Dome of the Rock. Fulcher of Chartres, for example, the chaplain of

These ornamented Crusader capitals grace the columns on the Crusader facade of the Church of the Holy Sepulchre.

Jerusalem's first Crusader king, Baldwin I (1100–1118), describes the Europeans' reaction to the rock in the midst of the Temple:

> They claimed to know by divination that the Ark of the Covenant of the Lord with the urn and with the tablets of Moses were enclosed and sealed in it [es-Sakhra]. Josiah, King of Judah, ordered it to be placed there, saying: "You will in no wise carry it from that place."[12]

Other writers state that the seven golden lamps of the Temple, the rod of Aaron, the altar of Jacob, the head of Zechariah and the urn of manna were physically present in the Templum Domini.[13]

Such references to relics mentioned in the Old Testament, however, largely disappear from the accounts after the first few years of Crusader rule. Instead, the later Crusader accounts associate the Dome of the Rock and its environs with the divine presence itself. The Crusaders even made this association concrete by altering the exterior of the Templum Domini. On each face of the octagonal structure, they added a Latin mosaic inscription taken from the liturgy that was commonly used for the dedication of a church. Proceeding counterclockwise from the Temple's west face, the inscriptions read:

Eternal peace on this House be from God the Lord
   eternally.
The temple of the Lord is holy, God's labor and
   sanctification.
This is the House of the Lord, firmly built.
Lord, in thy House all praise thy glory.
Blessed be the glory of the Lord from this Holy Place.
Blessed are they who dwell in thy House, O Lord.
Truly the Lord is in this place, and I did not know it.
Well founded is the House of the Lord on a firm rock.[14]

Unlike earlier Christians, who associated the Temple Mount
with Jesus' prophecy about the destruction of the Temple, the
Crusaders emphasized the continuity of tradition—from the earlier to the later dispensation, from the Old Testament Jewish
Temple to the Christian Templum Domini (Dome of the Rock).
If the Templum Domini was not the Jewish Temple, at least it
occupied the site where the biblical Temple had stood: It signi-
fied the completion and fulfillment of the Old Law.

It is not surprising, then, that the Crusaders connected the
Templum Domini with a particular passage in the Gospels: the
presentation of Christ. In this story,
when Mary and Joseph present
Jesus in the Jerusalem Temple, a
"righteous and devout" man
named Simeon recognizes the
youth as the Messiah. Simeon takes
Jesus in his arms, praises God and
declares to the congregation that
Jesus is "a light for revelation to the
Gentiles / and for glory to your
people Israel" (Luke 2:22–38).

**Once Saladin conquered Jerusalem, he
purged the Temple Mount/Haram al-Sharif
of all vestiges of the Crusader presence.
These braided Crusader columns, now in secondary use in a Muslim school, may have
been taken from one of the cloisters built by
Crusaders on the Temple Mount.**

Here the Crusaders were following medieval theologians in understanding the presentation of Christ as a nexus between the Old and New Covenants. Simeon, who serves God under the Old Law, recognizes in Jesus the incarnation of the New Law.

Inside the Templum Domini, the Crusaders hung a painting of the presentation of Christ. Accompanying the painting was a rhymed Latin inscription:

> The Virgin's Son, presented here,
> The King of Kings, the boy most dear,
> He makes this spot a holy place,
> And this most rightly is the case.
> The ladder Jacob saw was near
> The altar he erected here
> This memory makes more precious yet
> The holy place in which it's set.[15]

As the poem suggests, such a "holy place" was the setting for other sacred events. The great rock inside the Templum Domini, for instance, was the stone pillow on which Jacob rested his head while he dreamed of the ladder climbed by God's angels—again, like the Templum Domini, a meeting point of heaven and earth. One of the mosaic inscriptions on the Templum Domini ("Truly the Lord is in this place, and I did not know it") consists of the very words spoken by Jacob when he awoke from his dream (Genesis 28:16).[16]

The grotto within the rock, reached by a stairway from the south side of the choir, was regarded as the "sanctuary of the Lord"—the place where the angel Gabriel announced the conception of John the Baptist to his father, the priest Zechariah (Luke 1:5–20). Somewhat incongruously, this cave was also believed to be the spot where Jesus absolved the adulteress; thus it became a pilgrimage destination where supplicants came to confess their sins.[17]

The Dome of the Chain, the open kiosk to the east of the temple, was consecrated as a chapel of St. James the Less (also called James the Just). This James, the eldest of Jesus' four brothers, became the leader of the Jerusalem church in the years after

Jesus was crucified. In 62 A.D. he was martyred by being cast
down from the southeastern pinnacle of the Temple (other reports
say that he was stoned to death). An inscription marked the building as his tomb:

> Speak, stone and tomb, and answer those
> Who ask, "Whose bones do you enclose?"
> "They are of James the Just. He lies beneath
> This old memorial place of death."[18]

The actual physical appropriation of the buildings of the
Haram for Christian purposes seems to have been accomplished
rather quickly after the conquest of the city. Fulcher of Chartres
writes that only a week after the capture of the city, clergymen
were installed "to serve in the Church of the Lord's Sepulchre
and in His Temple."[19] The architectural adaptation of the Templum Domini for the Latin Christian rite seems to have taken
a bit longer. Fulcher describes the transformation of the interior: "In the middle of the Temple ... [was] a certain native rock
[es-Sakhra] ... Since that rock disfigured the Temple of the Lord,
afterwards it was entirely covered and encased in marble. Its
present position is under the altar where the priest performs
the rituals."[20]

Further alterations to the Templum Domini are recorded only
in later pilgrim accounts. A splendid wrought-iron screen stood
around the circumference of the inner arcade, separating the choir
from the laity; this screen was attested in about 1150, so it was
probably associated with the formal dedication of the building in
1142.[21] The cloister of the Augustinian canons was apparently well
established by 1154, when an Arab visitor admired its luxuriant
garden with all manner of trees.[22]

Sometime before 1170, a large gilt iron cross was erected over
the Dome. This constituted by far the most visible and weighty
symbol of Christian domination, and its significance was not lost
on the Muslim population, as a pilgrim to Jerusalem recorded:

> The sign of the Holy Cross has been fixed to the top by
> Christians, which is annoying to the Saracens. They would

be very glad to see it taken down, and have offered much of their own money. For even though they do not hold the faith in the passion of Christ they still revere this Temple, and wish to worship their Creator there.[23]

Jerusalem's Muslims extracted symbolic revenge after Saladin's conquest of the city; they dragged the cross through the streets to the Tower of David, where Jerusalem's Crusader kings had resided, and melted it down.[24]

By the time Saladin captured the city in 1187, Imad ad-Din had described extensive additions to the interior of the Dome of the Rock:

They had adorned it with images and statues, set up dwellings there for monks and made it the place for the Gospel, which they venerated and exalted to the heights. Over the place of the Prophet's holy foot they set an ornamented tabernacle with columns of marble, marking it as the place where the Messiah had set his foot; a holy and exalted place, where flocks of animals, among which I saw species of pig, were carved in marble.[25]

Several pieces of Crusader sculpture survive within the present Dome of the Rock, including the lintel over the portal leading down to the grotto. Other carvings, such as an octagonal tabernacle like the one described by Imad ad-Din, survive in the Minbar (Pulpit) of Qadi Burhan ad-Din, south of the temple.[26] These remains are too few and too jumbled in their reuse to show us how they were originally used, but it is clear that in Crusader times the Templum Domini's rich Islamic decoration was overlaid with numerous Romanesque sculptures.

One intact Crusader structure is the Qubbat al-Miraj (Dome of the Ascension), just northwest of the Dome of the Rock. According to an Arabic inscription on its lintel, it was erected in 1200/1201 by the Muslims, but the capitals appear to be Crusader work of the 1140s or 1150s.[27] The architectural evidence suggests that the structure was originally an open pavilion, which was subsequently walled in and furnished with a *mihrab* (the niche faced by Muslims when they pray) on its south side

No one really knows the original purpose of the Dome of the Ascension. Probably built around the time of the formal dedication of the Templum Domini in 1142, it has been conventionally described as a baptistery. However, there is no record of a baptistery associated with the Templum Domini, nor should we expect to find a baptistery associated with what was a commemorative shrine, not a church.[28]

In contrast to the Templum Domini, the Templum Salomonis does not seem to have been a pilgrimage site. The Al-Aqsa Mosque, as the Crusaders found it, was a very large congregational mosque.[29] Immediately following the conquest, it served as the palace of the Latin kings of Jerusalem, and it continued as the royal dwelling even after Baldwin II gave part of it to the newly founded Templar Knights in 1119.[30] In 1128 Pope Honorius II officially recognized the knights as a military order, and they adopted a rule written for them by St. Bernard of Clairvaux. At that time the royal palace was moved to the Tower of David, and the Templars gained the whole mosque for their headquarters.[31] The mosque itself was used as the Templars' living quarters, and the Umayyad substructures under the platform, "Solomon's Stables," were used for their horses.[32]

In the southeast corner of the Haram, near the Templum Salomonis, were two commemorative spots. The first was the corner itself, known to Christian pilgrims as the Pinnacle of the Temple, where Jesus was tempted by Satan (see Matthew 4:5–7; Luke 4:9–12) and where St. James the Less was cast down to his death. Beneath this was a shrine, recorded as the "Mosque of Mary" in several Arab sources predating the Crusader conquest, evidently a Muslim shrine that was taken over for Christian use after 1099.[33]

The Crusader alterations to the Al-Aqsa Mosque were extensive, but they are very difficult to sort out amid the later rebuildings and restorations. During the early years of Crusader rule, the building languished in a sad state of disrepair. The Templars, however, with their vast revenues from land holdings in Europe and the Levant, began a veritable building boom. A contemporary describes additions made by the knights in the 1170s:

On the other side of the palace, that is on the west, the Templars have built a new house, whose height, length and breadth, and all its cellars and refectories, staircase and roof, are far beyond the custom of this land ... There indeed they have constructed a new Palace, just as on the other side they have the old one. There too they have founded on the edge of the outer court a new church of magnificent size and workmanship.[34]

Although the additions erected on the east side of Al-Aqsa, including the church, were destroyed by Saladin, the buildings occupying the southwest corner of the Haram, including the knights' refectory, largely survive in the present Jami an-Nisa (Women's Mosque) and the Jami al-Maghariba (Moor's Mosque). The Al-Aqsa Mosque itself also preserves a sculpture produced in the last two decades of Crusader rule by a sculptural workshop probably associated with the Temple Mount. For example, an entire rose window is preserved in the Mihrab Zakariyya, a chapel of Crusader workmanship on the east side of the mosque. In a room below the *mihrab*, the *dikka* (a rostrum used for Koranic readings) is composed almost entirely of Crusader spolia (material plundered from Crusader buildings), including what may be columns from the cloister of the Templars' garden.[35]

One pervasive motif used by Crusader sculptors is the braided double column. This motif, which is found in both Byzantine and Romanesque art, was associated with the bronze pillars, called Jachin and Boaz, that Solomon erected at the portal of the First Temple (1 Kings 7:13–22).[36] Many pairs of such columns appear as spolia in the extant gates and fountains of the Haram. These braided columns were probably used as supports for cloisters on the Temple Mount, perhaps the cloister of the Augustinian canons at the Templum Domini or that of the Templars' court at the Templum Salomonis.[37] Their association with King Solomon, much like the Latin inscriptions on the Templum Domini, asserted the Christians' claim to be the legitimate successors of ancient Israel. The braided-column motif also appeared as part of the decoration on the Tomb of King Baldwin V (1185–1186), which stood in the Holy Sepulchre until the church was destroyed by fire in 1808. Here, too, a Latin king is associated with a Davidic king.

The Muslim reconquest of the city holds up an intriguing mirror to the Crusader occupation. After Saladin expelled the Franks from Jerusalem, Imad ad-Din tells us, he converted a number of the more important churches and monasteries into *madrassas* (schools) for the teaching of Islamic law and convents for Sufi mystics. The sultan was unsure what to do about the Church of the Holy Sepulchre, however. Some of his advisors urged him to destroy it completely, but wiser voices prevailed:

> Demolishing and destroying it would serve no purpose, nor would it prevent the infidels from visiting it or prevent their having access to it. For it is not the building as it appears to the eyes but the home of the Cross and Sepulchre that is the object of worship. The various Christian races would still be making pilgrimages here even if the earth had been dug up and thrown into the sky.[38]

So it was for the Crusaders. Regardless of how many times the Templum Domini had been leveled and rebuilt, it was at once Solomon's Temple and the Temple of Christ's Presentation.

Notes

1. Francesco Gabrieli, ed., *Arab Historians of the Crusades: Selected and Translated from the Arabic Sources* (Berkeley: Univ. of California Press, 1969), p. 169.

2. Gabrieli, *Arab Historians*, pp. 171–172.

3. See Priscilla Soucek, "The Temple of Solomon in Islamic Legend and Art," in *The Temple of Solomon: Archaeological Fact and Medieval Tradition in Christian, Islamic and Jewish Art*, ed. Joseph Gutmann (Missoula, MT: Scholars Press, 1976).

4. Raymond of Aguilers, chaplain to the Count of Toulouse, in Edward Peters, ed., *The First Crusade: The Chronicle of Fulcher of Chartres and Other Source Materials* (Philadelphia: Univ. of Pennsylvania Press, 1971), p. 214.

5. Myriam Rosen-Ayalon, "The Early Islamic Monuments of al-Haram al-Sharif: An Iconographic Study," *Qedem* 28 (Jerusalem: Institute of Archaeology, Hebrew Univ., 1989), p. 44.

6. John Wilkinson, ed., *Jerusalem Pilgrimage, 1099–1185* (London: Hakluyt Society, 1988), p. 173.

7. Wilkinson, *Pilgrimage*, p. 28.

8. Camille Enlart, *Les monuments des Croisés dans le Royaume de Jérusalem: Architecture religieuse et civile*, vol. 2 (Paris: Geuthner, 1928), p. 208.

9. Wilkinson, *Pilgrimage*, p. 104.

10. Wilkinson, *Pilgrimage*, p. 199.

11. Peter the Deacon, "Book on the Holy Places," in Wilkinson, *Pilgrimage*, p. 212.

12. Peters, *First Crusade*, p. 74.

13. For example, the "Ottobonian Guide" of c. 1103 and the guide known by its incipit *Qualiter*, in Wilkinson, *Pilgrimage*, pp. 91–92.

14. Two transcriptions of the texts exist, one by John of Würzburg and another by Theoderic. I follow Theoderic's order for the inscriptions (Wilkinson, *Pilgrimage*, pp. 289–290).

15. Wilkinson, *Pilgrimage*, p. 246.

16. A more scripturally savvy author found fault with this commemoration, pointing out that the vision of Jacob took place at Bethel, well north of Jerusalem. The author in question is John of Würzburg (Wilkinson, *Pilgrimage*, pp. 291, 247).

17. Wilkinson, *Pilgrimage*, pp. 247, 292.

18. Wilkinson, *Pilgrimage*, p. 292.

19. Peters, *First Crusade*, p. 79.

20. Peters, *First Crusade*, p. 74.

21. Bernard Hamilton, "Rebuilding Zion: The Holy Places of Jerusalem in the Twelfth Century," *Studies in Church History* 14 (Oxford and Cambridge, MA: Blackwell Publishers for the Ecclesiastical History Society, 1977), p. 110.

22. Marie Louis de Mas-Latrie, *Chronique d'Ernoul et de Bernard le Trésorier*, Publications de la Société de l'Histoire de France, 157 (Paris, 1871), p. 497.

23. Wilkinson, *Pilgrimage*, p. 249.

24. Mas-Latrie, *Chronique*, pp. 234–235.

25. Gabrieli, *Arab Historians*, p. 169.

26. Zehava Jacoby, "The Workshop of the Temple Area in Jerusalem in the Twelfth Century: Its Origin, Evolution and Impact," *Zeitschrift für Kunstgeschichte* 45 (Berlin: Deutscher Kunstverlag, 1982), p. 328; Helmut Buschhausen, *Die süditalienische Bauplastik im Königreich Jerusalem, Denkschriften der Österreichischen Akademie der Wissenschaften* 108 (Vienna, 1979), p. 225.

27. Jaroslav Folda, *Art of the Crusaders in the Holy Land: 1098–1187* (Cambridge: Cambridge Univ. Press, 1995), p. 253.

28. Folda, *Art of the Crusaders*, p. 253; cf. Enlart, *Monuments*, p. 212.

29. Keppel Archibald Cameron Creswell, *A Short Account of Early Muslim Architecture*, 2nd ed. (Missoula, MT: Scholars Press, 1989), p. 77.

30. Hamilton, "Rebuilding Zion," p. 110.

31. Enlart, *Monuments*, p. 216.

32. Wilkinson, *Pilgrimage*, p. 45.

33. Wilkinson, *Pilgrimage*, pp. 43, 295.

34. Wilkinson, *Pilgrimage*, p. 294.

35. Enlart, *Monuments*, pl. 115.

36. Walter Cahn, "Solomonic Elements in Romanesque Art," in Gutmann, *Temple of Solomon*, p. 51.

37. Jacoby, "Workshop," pp. 377–378.

38. Gabrieli, *Arab Historians*, pp. 174–175.

CHAPTER 3

✠

Was Jesus Buried Beneath the Church of the Holy Sepulchre?

DAN BAHAT

For many Christians, the most sacred place on earth is the Church of the Holy Sepulchre in Jerusalem. According to tradition, the church was built in the fourth century over both Golgotha (or Calvary), where Jesus was crucified, and the tomb where Jesus was buried. If the tradition is accurate, the Church of the Holy Sepulchre thus encloses sites associated with two of the most important events in Christianity: the crucifixion and the resurrection.

Not much remains of the fourth-century church, however. The structure we see was largely the work of the Crusaders, who rebuilt the Church of the Holy Sepulchre in the early 12th century.

Since 1960, the Armenian, Greek and Latin religious communities that are responsible for the care of the Holy Sepulchre Church in Jerusalem have been engaged in a joint restoration project. In connection with the restoration, they have undertaken extensive archaeological work to establish the history of the building and the site on which it rests. Thirteen trenches were excavated primarily to check the stability of Crusader structures, but these trenches also constituted archaeological excavations. Stripping plaster from the walls revealed structures from earlier periods. A new, modern drainage system was put in place, but the work itself was also used for archaeological research. Elsewhere, soundings were made for purely archaeological purposes.[1]

The two domes of the Church of the Holy Sepulchre loom above Jerusalem's Old City. The larger dome to the right is built over the traditional—and very possibly the actual—tomb of Jesus.

From these excavations, we now know a good deal about this important site.

During the late Judean monarchy, beginning in about the seventh or eighth century B.C., the area where the Holy Sepulchre Church is now located was a large limestone quarry. The city itself lay to the southeast and expanded first westward and then northward only at a later date. The high-quality limestone (known as meleke-type limestone) has been found wherever the excavations in the church reached bedrock. Traces of the quarry have been found not only in excavations of the church area, but also in excavations conducted nearby in the 1960s and 1970s, in the Muristan enclave of the Christian Quarter and in the Church of the Redeemer. This meleke stone was chiseled out in squarish blocks for building purposes. The cut rock surface that remains reveals to the archaeologist that the area was originally a quarry. Sometimes the workers left partially cut ashlars (shaped stones used in building) still attached to the bedrock. In one area (east of St. Helena's Chapel in the Holy Sepulchre Church), the quarry was over 40 feet deep. The earth and ash that filled the quarry contained pottery from about the seventh century B.C.; so the quarry can be securely dated.[2]

According to one of the site's principal excavators and the author of the excavation report, Father Virgilio C. Corbo, this quarry continued to be used until the first century B.C. At that time it was filled in and then covered with a layer of reddish-brown soil mixed with stone flakes from the ancient quarry. The quarry became a garden or orchard, where cereals, fig trees, carob trees and olive trees grew. As evidence of the garden, Father Corbo relies on the fact that above the quarry he found a layer of arable soil.[3] At this same time, the quarry-garden also became a cemetery. At least four tombs dating from this period have been found.

The first is the tomb traditionally known as the tomb of Nicodemus and Joseph of Arimathea. The Gospel accounts (John 19:38-41; Luke 23:50-53; Matthew 27:51-61) report that Joseph took Jesus' body down from the cross; Nicodemus brought myrrh and aloes; and then Joseph and Nicodemus wrapped Jesus' body in linen and buried him in a garden in Joseph's newly cut, rock-hewn tomb.

The tomb traditionally attributed to Joseph of Arimathea is a typical *kokh* (plural, *kokhim*) of the first century. *Kokhim* are long, narrow recesses cut perpendicularly into the wall of a burial cave. A coffin or the body of the deceased would be laid in such a recess. Or sometimes ossuaries (stone boxes in which the deceased's bones were placed about a year after the original burial) were placed in *kokhim*.

In the course of restoration work in the Holy Sepulchre Church, a hitherto unknown passage to this tomb was found beneath the rotunda.

Another type of tomb, known as an *arcosolium* was also common in this period. An *arcosolium* is a shallow niche cut in a burial tomb parallel to the wall; the top of an *arcosolium* is shaped like an arch, from which its name is derived. The so-called

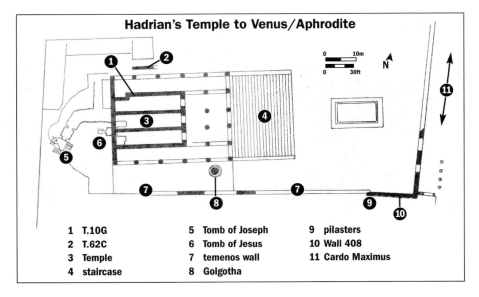

Hadrian's Temple to Venus/Aphrodite

1 T.10G	5 Tomb of Joseph	9 pilasters
2 T.62C	6 Tomb of Jesus	10 Wall 408
3 Temple	7 temenos wall	11 Cardo Maximus
4 staircase	8 Golgotha	

tomb of Jesus is composed of an antechamber and a rock-cut *arcosolium*. Unfortunately, centuries of pilgrims have completely deformed this tomb by chipping away bits of rock for souvenirs. Today the tomb is completely covered with later masonry, but enough is known to date it as an *arcosolium* from about the turn of the era.

A third, much larger tomb was found in front of the church (in the parvis). This tomb was greatly enlarged in Constantine's time and was used as a cistern. Although very little of it remains, there is enough to tell us that it originally functioned as a tomb. And in the late 19th century another tomb of the *kokh* type was found in the church area under the Coptic convent.[4]

Obviously other tombs that existed in the area were destroyed by later structures. But the evidence seems clear that at the turn of the era, this area was a large burial ground.

The tomb in front of the Church was actually cut into the rock of what is traditionally regarded as the hill of Golgotha, where Jesus was crucified. It is possible that the rocky outcrop of Golgotha was a memorial monument. However, this hypothesis needs more study before it can be advanced with any confidence.

The next period for which we have archaeological evidence in the Holy Sepulchre Church is from the period of the Roman emperor Hadrian. In 70 A.D. the Romans crushed the First Jewish Revolt; at that time they destroyed Jerusalem and burned the Temple. Less than 70 years later, in 132 A.D., the Jews again revolted, this time under the leadership of Rabbi Akivah and Bar Kokhba. It took the Romans three years to suppress the Second Jewish Revolt. This time, however, the victorious Roman emperor Hadrian banned Jews from Jerusalem. To remove every trace of its Jewish past, Hadrian rebuilt Jerusalem as a Roman city named Aelia Capitolina. (For the same reason, he also changed the name of the country from Judea to Palaestina or Palestine.)

On the site of the former seventh-century B.C. quarry and first-century B.C. orchard-garden and cemetery, where the Holy Sepulchre Church was to be built, Hadrian constructed a gigantic raised platform, which consisted of a nearly rectangular retaining wall filled with earth. On top of the platform, he built a smaller raised podium, and on top of the podium, he built a temple.

Many of the ashlars (shaped stones) used by Hadrian for the retaining wall of the platform were actually old Herodian ashlars, left after the Roman destruction of Jerusalem and Herod's temple in 70 A.D. They are identical in size and facing to the Herodian ashlars in the retaining wall of the Temple Mount. The fact that Hadrian appears to have deliberately attempted to duplicate the Herodian enclosure at the Temple Mount has special significance. According to the fourth-century church historian Eusebius of Caesarea (in present-day northern Israel), Hadrian built an elaborate temple to the goddess Venus/Aphrodite on his platform—perhaps deliberately in opposition to what the Romans saw as the local cult of Yahweh. A number of fifth-century sources also refer to a temple of Venus/Aphrodite on the site where the Church of the Holy Sepulchre was later built.

Queen Helena, the mother of Rome's first Christian emperor, Constantine, was shown the site on her visit to Jerusalem in 326 A.D. We know little about the condition of the site at this time. Perhaps Hadrian's temple was already in ruins—destroyed by zealous Christians.

After Queen Helena's visit, the Christian community removed whatever remained of the Hadrianic temple, as well as the Hadri-

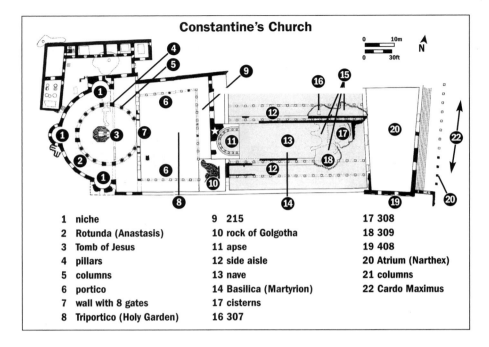

Constantine's Church

1	niche	9	215	17	308
2	Rotunda (Anastasis)	10	rock of Golgotha	18	309
3	Tomb of Jesus	11	apse	19	408
4	pillars	12	side aisle	20	Atrium (Narthex)
5	columns	13	nave	21	columns
6	portico	14	Basilica (Martyrion)	22	Cardo Maximus
7	wall with 8 gates	17	cisterns		
8	Triportico (Holy Garden)	16	307		

anic enclosure and the fill it contained. For the Christian community, this fill, intended by Hadrian to create a level surface for building, represented Hadrian's attempt to obliterate forever Jesus' tomb and the rock of Golgotha, where he had been crucified.

According to literary sources (especially Eusebius's *Life of Constantine*), Constantine built a rotunda around Jesus' tomb. In front of the rotunda was the site of the crucifixion (Golgotha or Calvary), in what is referred to in ancient literary sources as the Holy Garden. On the other side of the garden, Constantine built a long church in the shape of a basilica, consisting of a nave and side aisles separated from the nave by rows of columns. Here the faithful could offer prayers. Between the rotunda and the basilica lay the hill of Golgotha.

Was the Constantinian rotunda actually built over the true site of Jesus' burial? Although we can never be certain, it seems very likely that it was.

As we have seen, the site was a turn-of-the-era cemetery. The cemetery, including Jesus' tomb, had itself been buried for nearly

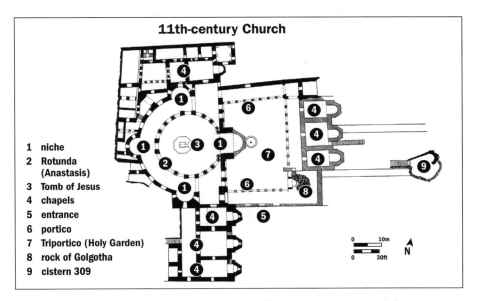

11th-century Church

1 niche
2 Rotunda (Anastasis)
3 Tomb of Jesus
4 chapels
5 entrance
6 portico
7 Triportico (Holy Garden)
8 rock of Golgotha
9 cistern 309

300 years. The fact that it had indeed been a cemetery, and that this memory of Jesus' tomb survived despite Hadrian's construction project, suggests the authenticity of the site. Moreover, the fact that the Christian community in Jerusalem was never dispersed during this period (the succession of bishops was never interrupted) supports the accuracy of the preserved memory that Jesus had been crucified and buried here.

Perhaps the strongest argument in favor of the authenticity of the site, however, is that it must have been regarded as an unlikely location when pointed out to Queen Helena in the fourth century. Then, as now, the site lay in a crowded urban setting—which would have been a strange and revolting burial site for a fourth-century pilgrim. But we now know that its location perfectly fits first-century conditions.

By the fourth century, this site had long been enclosed within the city walls. The wall enclosing this part of the city (referred to by Josephus as the Third Wall) had been built by Herod Agrippa, the local ruler who governed Judea between 41 and 44 A.D. This wall, then, was built after Jesus' crucifixion—though not more than 10 or 15 years afterward. And that is the crucial point.

When Jesus was buried in about 30 A.D., this area was *outside* the city—a perfectly appropriate location, therefore, for burial tombs. But no one in 325 A.D. would have known that, unless, perhaps, the memory of Jesus' burial had been accurately preserved.

The Gospels tell us that Jesus was buried "near the city" (John 19:20); the site we are considering was then just outside the city, the city wall being only about 500 feet to the south and 350 feet to the east. We are also told the site was in a garden (John 19:41), which is at the very least consistent with the archaeological evidence we have of the first-century A.D. condition of the site.

The basilica Constantine built in front of the tomb was typical of its time. It consisted of a center nave and aisles on either side of the nave separated from the nave by rows of columns. At the far end of the nave was a single apse. Unfortunately, hardly a trace of Constantine's basilica remains. From sections of the wall that have been excavated, we can only confirm the basilica's location.

Behind (west of) Constantine's basilica was a large open gar-

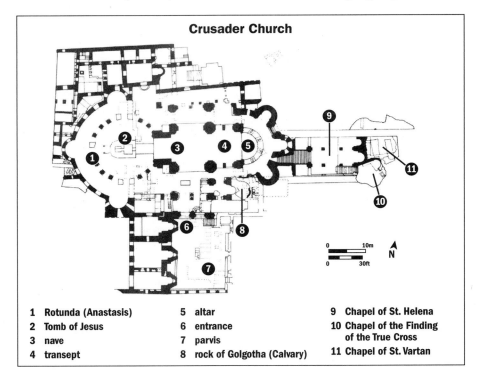

Crusader Church

0   10m
0   30ft
N

1	Rotunda (Anastasis)	5	altar	9	Chapel of St. Helena
2	Tomb of Jesus	6	entrance	10	Chapel of the Finding of the True Cross
3	nave	7	parvis		
4	transept	8	rock of Golgotha (Calvary)	11	Chapel of St. Vartan

den on the other side of which, in the rotunda, stood the tomb of Jesus. The apse of the basilica faced the tomb. The archaeological evidence suggests that the rotunda was probably part of the original Constantinian construction and design. Also, many temples to goddesses (like Venus/Aphrodite) are round, in the form of rotundas. If it is true, as Eusebius says, that Hadrian had built a temple to Venus/Aphrodite here, it was quite probably a round temple. The Christian rotunda may well have been inspired by this pagan rotunda. (The phenomenon of a holy site from one religion being maintained as holy by subsequent religions was common throughout the ancient world.) If the architecture of Hadrian's pagan rotunda inspired the rotunda around Jesus' tomb, it is more likely that the later rotunda was built by Constantine himself, not by a later ruler who would not have known the pagan rotunda.

Two original columns of the rotunda built around Jesus' tomb have been preserved. In *The Church of the Holy Sepulchre in Jerusalem* (Oxford University Press, 1974), one of the principal architects involved in the restoration, Father Charles Coüasnon, argues that this column had previously served in the portico of the Hadrianic temple; the two halves were later reused in the rotunda. In this, he is probably correct.

On the side of the niche that marked Jesus' tomb, a drain had been cut in the rock, apparently to allow rain water to drain from the tomb. This might indicate that at least for some time the tomb stood in the open air. How long we cannot know.

In any event, a rotunda was soon built around the tomb where the current reconstructed tomb—the focus of the present church—now stands. This rotunda is often referred to, both now and in historical records, as the Anastasis (Resurrection).

Between the rotunda and the basilica church was the Holy Garden, which was enclosed (probably only on three sides) by a portico set on a row of columns—creating a rectangular courtyard. Separating this porticoed courtyard from the rotunda was a wall with eight gates.

This complex—basilica, garden, rotunda and tomb—stood until the Persian invasion of 614 A.D. At that time it was damaged by fire, but not, as once supposed, totally destroyed. When the Persians conquered Jerusalem, they destroyed many of its churches, but not the Holy Sepulchre.

The situation was different, however, in 1009 A.D. On the order of the Fatimid caliph of Cairo, al-Hakim, the entire church complex was almost completely destroyed.

The basilica was gone forever, razed to the ground. Only the 1968 discovery of the foundation of the western apse of the basilica allows its placement to be fixed with certainty (though previous reconstructions had indeed fixed its location correctly).

The rotunda, however, was preserved to a height of about five feet. Between 1042 and 1048, the Byzantine emperor Constantine IX Monomachus attempted to restore the complex. He was most successful with the rotunda, which was restored with only slight change. Where the Constantinian rotunda had three niches on three sides, Monomachus added a fourth. This new niche was on the east side, the direction of prayer in most churches. The new niche was the largest of the niches and was no doubt the focus of prayer in the rotunda.

In front of the rotunda, Monomachus retained the open garden. One of the old colonnades (the northern one) was rebuilt by him and has been preserved to the present time, thus enabling us to study the character of Monomachus's restoration.

Instead of a basilica, Monomachus built three groups of chapels. One group, consisting of three chapels, abutted the old baptistery; a second group, also consisting of three chapels, was built near the site of the apse of the destroyed basilica (this group is known from historical documentation only); and the third consisted of a chapel north of the rotunda.

In the course of his reconstruction, Monomachus discovered a cistern where, he believed, Queen Helena had discovered the True Cross. This does not seem to have been an ancient tradition, however. The cistern dates to the 11th or 12th century, and nothing was built to commemorate Helena's supposed discovery of the True Cross until the Crusader period—such as the famous Chapel of St. Helena, which the Crusaders built adjacent to the cistern.

The Crusaders, who ruled Jerusalem from 1099 to 1187, rebuilt the church essentially in the form we know it today. The rotunda (or Anastasis) enclosing the tomb was maintained as the focus of the new structure. In the area of the porticoed garden in front of the rotunda, the Crusaders built a nave with a transept, forming a cross, and installed a high altar.

The traditional rock of Golgotha, where Jesus had been crucified, was enclosed—for the first time—in this Crusader church. In Hadrian's time, the rock of Golgotha had protruded above the Hadrianic enclosure-platform. According to the Christian scholar St. Jerome (c. 342-420), a statue of Venus/Aphrodite was set on top of the protruding rock. This statue was no doubt removed by Christians who venerated the rock. When Constantine built his basilica, the rock was squared to fit into a chapel in the southeast corner of the Holy Garden.

The Crusaders enclosed the rock in a chapel within the church itself. The floor level of this chapel, where the rock may still be seen, is almost at the height of the top of the rock. Because of this, a lower chapel, named for Adam, was installed to expose the lower part of the rock. This lower chapel served as a burial chapel in the 12th century for the Crusader kings of the Kingdom of Jerusalem.

The Church of the Holy Sepulchre has thus been sanctified ground for 2,000 years. It has actually been a series of holy sites— a cemetery, a temple to the Greco-Roman love goddess, Byzantine basilicas and a Crusader church. Today it is a vast complex of rooms and chapels, testifying to the widespread nature of Christianity and the vigor of tradition.

Notes

1. The results of this excavation and research are published in a three-volume final report by Virgilio C. Corbo, *Il Santo Sepolcro di Gerusalemme, Aspetti archeologici dalle origini al periodo crociato* (1981-1982), professor of archaeology at the Studium Biblicum Franciscanum in Jerusalem. Although the text itself (volume 1) is in Italian, there is a 16-page English summary by Stanislao Loffreda. Father Loffreda has also translated into English the captions to the archaeological drawings and reconstructions (volume II) and the archaeological photographs (volume III).

2. See Magen Broshi, "Recent Excavations in the Church of the Holy Sepulchre," *Qadmoniot*, Vol. 10, No. 1, 1977, pp. 30ff. (in Hebrew). More recently, see Magen Broshi and Gabriel Barkay, "Excavations in the Chapel of St. Vartan in the Holy Sepulchre," *Israel Exploration Journal* 35, Nos. 1-3 (1985), p. 108ff.

3. Broshi and Barkay do not mention this layer of arable soil; instead they found an Iron Age II floor of beaten earth above the quarry fill. Based on this floor and the large

quantities of Iron Age B pottery found below, in and above this floor, they conclude this area was residential from the late eighth century to the Babylonian destruction of Jerusalem. They date the quarry mainly to the ninth-eighth centuries B.C. before the city expanded into this extramural area in the late eighth century. Corbo contends that this floor cannot be dated to Iron Age II.

4. Conrad Schick, "Notes from Jerusalem," *Palestine Exploration Fund Quarterly Statement*, 1887, pp. 156-170.

⛭

CHAPTER 4

The Holy Sepulchre on an Ancient Gold Ring

YAAKOV MESHORER

A gold ring was found in 1974 in the excavations south of the Temple Mount in Jerusalem. At the time, the suggestion that the ring depicted the Holy Sepulchre, or tomb of Jesus, met with considerable scholarly skepticism. The ring has never been studied or published. My own view is that the structure on the ring does in fact represent the Holy Sepulchre.

Although the ring was uncovered in an excavation, the locus and level of the find give no indication as to its date. The ring must therefore be dated principally on the basis of its style.

Similar rings are also known from several other collections. An almost identical ring, for example, can be found at the Benaki Museum in Athens. Others have been found in Israel as well as in Europe, which, as we shall see, suggests they were brought back from the Holy Land by Crusaders.

The shape of the structure depicted imitates the features of a particular building, not simply a building in general. But what building? Let us look at the ring and its building more closely.

The structure mounted on the ring is square. It has a cone-shaped cupola on top. On each facade is a large round vault. In the center of each of the four round vaults is a shaft with two branches at the bottom. The round vaults are composed of gold granulation.

The cupola on top of the structure is made of long strips, joined at the top by a ring. On top of the cupola ring is a knob. On the lower part of the cupola are two rows of perforations, or holes, that alternate above one another. A zigzag line runs between perforations.

The ring itself, through which the finger fits, is granulated on its edges. A wavy line meanders around the center part of the ring.

It is my impression that the ring is Christian because of the design of the vaults. The shaft with two branches resembles a stylized lily with a long central petal reaching the top of the vault; each side of the structure is divided in half by this stylized lily, which creates in effect two vaulted sections. The lily was a well-known Christian symbol during the Crusader period, so the edifice depicted on the ring therefore probably represents an important Christian building of the Crusader period.

There is a remarkable similarity between the structure on the ring and a representation of the Crusader Holy Sepulchre from the church itself. This Crusader Holy Sepulchre is depicted on marble screens once adorning the facade of the church. Now housed in the Rockefeller Museum in Jerusalem, these screens depict the Holy Sepulchre as a cone-shaped cupola with a knob at the top and perforations at the bottom (see photo, opposite), just like the structure on our ring.

The connection between the ring and the Holy Sepulchre is also suggested by an engraving (see photo, p. 38) made in 1483 by the German artist Bernhard von Breydenbach. The dome and open vaults on the ring resemble the structure built on top of Jesus' tomb enclosure in the engraving.

Accordingly, I believe that this ring probably depicts the Holy

A stylized lily—a shaft with two branches at its base—divides each round vault on the four sides of this golden ring. The lily form was a familiar Christian symbol during the Crusader period.

A marble screen from a lintel in the facade of the Crusader Church of the Holy Sepulchre depicts a structure similar to that on the gold ring. Above the heads, at the intersection of the two curved moldings, is a cone-shaped cupola topped by a knob; open arches are visible below the cupola. The structure resembles the dome and knob on the gold ring—and thus perhaps the domed superstructure of Jesus' tomb in the Church of the Holy Sepulchre.

Sepulchre, or tomb of Jesus, within the church rotunda as it was seen in the Church of the Holy Sepulchre during the Crusader period. The fact that such rings have been found both in Jerusalem and in Europe tends to support this identification.

Rings with buildings on them are well known from the 15th and 16th centuries. The most popular ones were Jewish wedding rings that showed various buildings of European style and were sometimes inscribed with the Hebrew inscription *mazel tov* ("good luck").

In this 1483 engraving by the German artist Bernhard von Breydenbach, the aedicule (tomb enclosure) bears a dome supported on open vaults. It seems likely that the gold ring depicts such a domed superstructure that stood in the rotunda of the Crusader Church of the Holy Sepulchre—or possibly the dome of the rotunda itself.

Ring makers in Jerusalem likely copied this concept for Christian pilgrims visiting Jerusalem; such rings featured the Holy Sepulchre and were very probably sold as souvenirs in the 15th and 16th centuries. In this way, some of the rings made their way to Europe. Others, like this one, remained in Jerusalem, to be uncovered centuries later by archaeologists.

CHAPTER 5

Jerusalem in Bologna

*Another Crusader Church
of the Holy Sepulchre*

ROBERT OUSTERHOUT

S hould you want to visit the Crusader Church of the Holy
Sepulchre, don't go to Jerusalem.[1] The Jerusalem church will
just confuse you.

The modern pilgrim, expecting to see the sites of Jesus' crucifixion, entombment and resurrection, usually comes away from
the church in Jerusalem more perplexed than reassured. Questions of authenticity mix with general bewilderment as crowds
of the faithful stumble through the rabbit warren of historic
rebuildings, scaffoldings and subdivisions, cluttered with relics,
oversized candlesticks and overwhelmingly mediocre art. It is no
wonder that in the 19th century, General Charles R. Gordon pro-
posed an alternative site for the Tomb of Jesus, the so-called Garden Tomb, in a tranquil spot outside the wall of Jerusalem's Old
City.[2] Although Gordan's alternative is not accepted today, the
Garden Tomb's restful seclusion does *seem* a more appropriate
location—which, in the words of biblical scholar Jerome Murphy-
O'Connor, "conforms to the expectations of simple piety."[3]

So here's my advice. If you want to see what the medieval Holy
Sepulchre looked like, go to Bologna—to the seven churches of
Santo Stefano. It's much simpler and far less disorienting. Besides,
you can't see the original building in Jerusalem anyway. It hasn't
survived. It has been reconstructed almost out of existence.

Begun by Constantine the Great in 326, the original Church
of the Holy Sepulchre was much simpler in design and decora-

tion than the present building. The church was constructed on the site of Jesus' crucifixion and burial—Calvary (also called Golgotha) and the tomb—as identified by Constantine's saintly mother, Helena. Constantine's biographer Eusebius describes the lavishly appointed church as "an illustrious memorial of the saving resurrection, bright with rich and royal splendor."[4]

But we have only an approximate idea of how the fourth-century building looked, thanks to images like the sixth-century Madaba mosaic map of Jerusalem.[5] We also have the descriptions of the complex recorded by early pilgrims and, most importantly, the details that have emerged from the archaeological explorations of the 1960s and 1970s, most convincingly explicated by Father Virgilio Corbo.[6]

The fourth-century complex enclosed the most significant holy sites (Calvary and the tomb) and established basic architectural features to glorify them. The entry to the vast complex of buildings was on the Cardo, the main colonnaded street of the city. An atrium or courtyard connected the Cardo to a large five-aisled basilica, or hall, with a wooden roof and an apse oriented to the west. Behind the basilica was a porticoed courtyard with the rock of Calvary in the southeast corner. Finally, at the western end of the complex, stood the great rotunda of the Anastasis (Resurrection), housing the aedicula, or shrine, of the Tomb of Christ.[7] In the Madaba map, the church is shown with a gabled roof and three doors opening on the facade. The golden dome of the rotunda over Jesus' tomb rises behind the basilica. The rotunda was actually D-shaped in plan, and its central space was surrounded by an ambulatory that broadened into transepts to the north and south. The aedicula itself was formed from a bedrock outcropping containing the rock-hewn tomb chamber; it had been left standing as the bedrock was quarried away around it and was subsequently decorated with marble to resemble a small temple.

Eusebius claimed that all remains of an earlier Roman temple had been removed to purify the site.[8] In fact, as Corbo has demonstrated, several Roman walls and foundations—relics of the earlier Roman temple—were incorporated into the Constantinian complex, and these help to explain its numerous irregularities.[9]

But the Constantinian complex has not survived. Following

damage and repair in the seventh and tenth centuries, about which little is known, the church was destroyed in 1009 by the fanatic Fatimid caliph al-Hakim, who was offended by the Easter ceremony of the Descent of the Holy Fire (in which a lighted lamp within the dark tomb of Jesus was believed to be a flame from heaven). Following the death of al-Hakim and decades of negotiations, the church was subsequently rebuilt with the financial support of the Byzantine emperor Constantine IX Monomachus and completed in 1048.

This reconstruction of the Holy Sepulchre, which adhered to Byzantine architectural ideas, was probably directed by a master mason from Constantinople.[10] Although the rotunda and the porticoed courtyard between the tomb and the basilica remained much the same, neither the basilica nor the atrium was reconstructed. The new Anastasis Rotunda, which was provided with an apse and enveloped by numerous annexed chapels, became the focal point of the complex. Although short-lived, this phase of the Holy Sepulchre was particularly influential throughout history, as we shall see, corresponding to a period of intensive contact between the Holy Land and Western Europe.

Only part of the building from this period survives. Following the conquest of Jerusalem at the completion of the First Crusade in 1099, the complex was given a more unified appearance in accordance with western European standards.[11] The Crusaders began by remodeling the tomb aedicula. Subsequently, the courtyard and its subsidiary chapels were replaced by a domed transept and a Romanesque pilgrimage choir (with an ambulatory and radiating chapels surrounding the apse, as at Santiago de Compostela in northern Spain). For the first time, all the holy sites were housed under one roof, with the monumental entrance at the south transept.

That's more or less the building we see today. The belfry lost its top in an earthquake in 1545—it fell onto the dome of a neighboring chapel, which remains unroofed. Subsequently, the upper two stories of the belfry were removed in the 18th century. Large parts of the complex were reconstructed following a major fire in 1808, and the aedicula of the tomb was entirely reconstructed. Stones damaged in the 19th-century fire have been systematically replaced in a massive ongoing restoration project.

There's an old joke that a camel is a horse designed by a committee. The Holy Sepulchre is a camel, a compromise between the three competing medieval planning concepts—Early Christian, Byzantine and Romanesque. In fact, the present plan is so filled with disquieting disjunctions and jarring juxtapositions that it was once all too appropriately included as an illustration in

GIOVANNI LATTANZI

A model tomb of Jesus stands just west of center in the rotunda of the Bologna church, reminiscent of the off-center tomb in the rotunda of the Church of Holy Sepulchre in Jerusalem. The Bologna tomb is apparently based on the structure that enclosed the tomb (called the aedicula) in the 11th-century Jerusalem church. But it is now difficult to enumerate the parallels, because the tomb of Jesus in the Holy Sepulchre Church was rebuilt by Crusaders in the 12th century, and the Bologna tomb has undergone many alterations (including the addition of the pulpit on the left side).

GARO NALBANDIAN

The tomb of Jesus stands near the center of the rotunda of the Church of Holy Sepulchre. The tomb's cupola, blackened by the smoke of worshiper's candles, rises above the inner tomb chamber, which contains an empty burial bench. The modern aedicula has little in common with the smaller, single-story shrine built by Constantine, although it does preserve architectural and design motifs from the series of shrines repeatedly built and rebuilt on this spot over the centuries.

Robert Venturi's seminal work on postmodernism, *Complexity and Contradiction in Architecture*.[12]

History provided one set of complications, modern usage another. The present interior of the building has been repeatedly subdivided by the various congregations it houses, so that the intended unity of the interior space is no longer evident. The ambulatory and gallery of the rotunda have been partitioned; the transepts of the Crusader choir have been walled off. The temporary partitions have now become permanent barriers, and within each sector of the building, new decorative elements proclaim the presence of special religious interests. The Crusaders' dome in the transept, for example, originally intended to be left plain, was recently decorated with Greek mosaics of questionable artistic merit. The pavement of the chapel of St. Helena now bears representations of the sacred shrines of Armenia, and the chapel has been given a new, complementary dedication to the martyrs of Armenia. A visit to the Holy Sepulchre today speaks of religious partisanship more than ecumenical unity.

And this brings us to Bologna and Santo Stefano. Located in a

quiet piazza just east of the *due torre*, the two tall medieval towers in the heart of the historic city, the church and monastery of
Santo Stefano (Saint Stephen) rest on one of the oldest foundations in Bologna. Rebuilt after 1141, apparently by returning Crusaders, the core of the *sette chiese* (seven churches) of Santo Stefano represents the most complete copy of the Holy Sepulchre to
survive from the Middle Ages.[13] Constructed of red brick decorated with the lively stone patterning characteristic of northern
Italy, the evocative image of Santo Stefano affirms both the site's
antiquity and its religious significance. Although augmented over
the centuries, the central churches of the complex clearly repli-
cate, in a smaller scale, the main monuments of Jerusalem, while
transforming them into an Italian Romanesque style.

The complex centers on the chapel of Santo Sepolcro, a copy
of Jerusalem's Anastasis Rotunda. Santo Sepolcro is an irregular
octagon in plan, topped by a brick cloister vault composed of
twelve flattened, wedge-shaped segments, with an internal colon-
nade of 12 supports. An extra column in the northeast is identified as the Column of the Flagellation, replicating a relic at the
Holy Sepulchre. The unusual marble monument in the center
of Santo Sepolcro is a much-reconstructed copy of the tomb aedicula. Its main facade is decorated with late medieval sculptures
of the Holy Women at the Tomb, and its low entrance is covered
by a grille. Inside, a cenotaph corresponds to the position of
the tomb of Jesus; opposite are the relics of the patron saint of
Bologna, San Petronio.

To the east of Santo Sepolcro lies a charming porticoed court,
a replica of the porticoed court in Jerusalem. The basin at its center was apparently originally kept elsewhere in the complex and
may have been used for the distribution of bread. However, it later
became associated with the basin in which Pontius Pilate washed
his hands. The court connects to a series of chapels: The central, cruciform chapel was dedicated to Santa Croce. Called Cal-
vario, it was said to contain "copies" of the Mount of Calvary and
of the True Cross, which were alleged to have been based on
measurements taken in Jerusalem. The distance between Calvary
and the tomb also corresponds to that at Jerusalem.

The *Vita* of San Petronio, written in 1180, proudly attributes

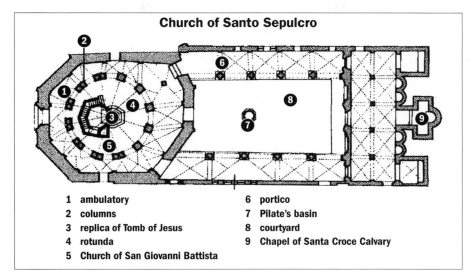

Church of Santo Sepulcro

1 ambulatory
2 columns
3 replica of Tomb of Jesus
4 rotunda
5 Church of San Giovanni Battista

6 portico
7 Pilate's basin
8 courtyard
9 Chapel of Santa Croce Calvary

the complex of Santo Stefano to the fifth-century patron saint of Bologna, claiming that he visited Jerusalem and returned with relics and measurements.[14] More likely, the Bologna copy was the result of the First Crusade of 1099 and was meant to reproduce the 11th-century form of the Holy Sepulchre, with rotunda, courtyard and chapels. We may assume that the alleged association with San Petronio was intended to add to its historical luster.

Other sites in Bologna purported to have been founded by San Petronio have special associations with Jerusalem, including the Church of San Giovanni in Monte Oliveti, which is said to imitate the Church of the Ascension on the Mount of Olives, and the Church of Santa Tecla, alleged to be a "copy" of the Valley of Josephat and of the Field of Hakeldama (Potter's Field). How a church could copy a valley or a field is not entirely clear; unfortunately, the church no longer survives. A Pool of Siloam is also mentioned. Evidently the intent was to establish an extensive topographical connection between Jerusalem and Bologna.

To be sure, the churches of Santo Stefano were not without their complexities, but the message of the medieval complex was nevertheless clear: This is Jerusalem transported to Bologna.

Geography was a flexible concept in the Middle Ages. The "Jerusalem" in Bologna wasn't simply a copy of the holy sites; it

GIOVANNI LATTANZI

A courtyard connects the Holy Sepulchre with the Chapel of Santa Croce Calvary (visible at upper left) in the Bologna church complex—much as in the Jerusalem church built by Constantine and then rebuilt in the 11th century. When the Crusaders once again rebuilt the Jerusalem church in the 12th century, however, they eliminated the courtyard. The inscription on the basin in the center of the courtyard—"filled with the supper of the Lord"—indicates that it originally stood indoors and held eucharistic bread. Only later was it associated with the basin in which Pilate washed his hands.

was believed that through the combination of image, dedications and devotional acts, the sacred topography of the Holy City could be relocated, re-created, as it were, at a new site. Bologna could become Jerusalem. This is how Santo Stefano was understood in the late Middle Ages.

The significance of Santo Stefano lay in the belief that sanctity or spiritual value could be associated with persons, places or objects, and that by being captured in matter, the numinous qualities could be carried away from the original location. Such transfers of holiness were common in the Middle Ages, although they were normally enacted on a smaller scale than our Bologna example, and were a routine component of Christian pilgrimage.[15]

Pilgrims to the Holy Land routinely returned with souvenirs— ampullae (flasks), amulets, pieces of stone or earth—all generally called in Greek *eulogiai*, or "blessings." A good example is a sixth-century tin-lead ampulla from the Dumbarton Oaks collection in Washington (see photo, p. 49), which is decorated with a scene of the Holy Women at the Sepulchre, the latter represented by a schematic rendition of the architecture of the Anastasis Rotunda and the tomb aedicula. According to its inscription, the ampulla originally contained oil from a lamp that burned at the tomb of Jesus. These "blessings" were believed to carry a portion of the sanctity of their point of origin, and the faithful believed that they could cure diseases, perform miracles and aid in salvation. Another sixth-century souvenir, a reliquary box from the Sancta Sanctorum in Rome, contains "blessings" in the form of rocks and earth from holy sites in Palestine. Its lid is decorated with scenes from the life of Christ.[16]

Related to this phenomenon was the practice of copying the architecture of holy sites, of which the "Jerusalem" in Bologna is perhaps the best-preserved example among many. The Holy Sepulchre was the most important Christian site and was thus copied dozens of times throughout western Europe during the Middle Ages.[17] Frequently the copies were built by returning pilgrims and Crusaders, aided by verbal descriptions, visual images and rudimentary plans or measurements taken on-site. The Bologna copy was no more than a "blessing"—a pilgrim's souvenir—of architectural dimension. The "Jerusalem" in Bologna was a sort of sacred stand-in that became the object of a pilgrimage by proxy. Indeed, visitors to copies of the Holy Sepulchre often received indulgences similar to those offered to Jerusalem pilgrims.

In most of the medieval European examples, only the Anastasis Rotunda was replicated. It was usually reduced in scale, simplified in form and reproduced in a local architectural style. At Neuvy-St.-Sépulcre in central France, for example, a rotunda was built in the 11th century by returning pilgrims. Like Santo Sepolcro at Santo Stefano, the French church was dedicated to the Holy Sepulchre and originally contained a copy of the tomb of Jesus and relics from Jerusalem.[18] Located on a major route to the tomb-shrine of St. James at Santiago de Compostela, in Spain, Neuvy became a popular "pilgrimage within a pilgrimage," allowing the medieval traveler to visit Jerusalem by proxy on the way to Santiago.

An architectural copy could also take on broader associations. For example, the rotunda of St. Michael at Fulda, in central Germany, originally constructed around 820 and rebuilt in the late

11th century, also seems to have been modeled after the Anastasis Rotunda and originally included a *tumulus*—a mound representing the tomb of Jesus. But it included relics from Bethlehem and Sinai as well.[19] Thus a reproduction of a single building forged an association with the entire Holy Land. In this instance, the copy functioned as a funeral chapel. The Jerusalem imagery thereby made spiritually present the life-giving powers of the tomb of Jesus; at the same time, the faithful of Fulda could be buried "in the Holy Land."

Medieval copies of the Holy Sepulchre served a variety of special functions that were enhanced by the architectural imitation. Neuvy was a pilgrimage church, Fulda a funeral chapel. Santo Stefano in Bologna was replete with distinctive services and ceremonies that were important components of life in medieval Bologna. The Bologna churches were the setting for special liturgical celebrations, such as a Palm Sunday procession that recreated Jesus' Entry into Jerusalem, apparently in imitation of services conducted in Jerusalem. The tomb aedicula in Santo Stefano may have been the setting for liturgical dramas during Easter that reenacted the entombment and resurrection.[20]

Although these ceremonies were no doubt important in and of themselves, they can also be understood in a civic context. The New Jerusalem in Bologna might be best understood in relation to urban development in Italy during the high Middle Ages. Jerusalem in its heavenly and earthly aspects was regarded as the ideal city in the Middle Ages. In the 11th and 12th centuries, the increased contact between western Europe and the Holy Land coincided with a period of rapid urbanization in the West. This period was also marked by the rebirth of civic consciousness. As urban entities attempted to define themselves, the image of Jerusalem, real and ideal, was incorporated into that definition. Throughout Italy, the emerging cities like Bologna were equated with Jerusalem or with Paradise. The medieval city could be simultaneously associated with both the heavenly and the earthly Jerusalem, and this is reflected in numerous writings and civic ceremonies of the period. As the city planners re-created the sacred topography of Jerusalem, the developing civic entity was mystically transformed into the ideal city.[21]

DUMBARTON OAKS, WASHINGTON DC

Pilgrims to the Holy Land used this tiny (less than 2 inches in diameter) tin-lead flask, decorated with an image of three women at the tomb, to carry home oil taken from the lamps hanging above Jesus' tomb. This sixth-century flask offers a rare image of the rotunda and tomb built by Constantine. Directly below the inscription (reading "the Lord is risen") is a row of windows cut into the dome of the rotunda, supported by four large columns. Between them stands Jesus' tomb, with its triangular gable. The crescent shape inside the door probably represents the low entryway of the inner tomb chamber; the slab on the ground may represent the stone that sealed the Tomb of Jesus.

With a trip to Bologna, you can thus visit both Jerusalem and Bologna at the same time—two for the price of one. Make a culinary pilgrimage to sample Bologna's famous North Italian cuisine and get a good impression of what the medieval Holy Sepulchre looked like. For the serious gourmand, expiation for the sin of gluttony can be sought straightaway with a pilgrimage to "Jerusalem," barely five minutes from the Piazza Maggiore.

The idea of a topographical transfer, as represented by the re-creation of Jerusalem in Bologna, also affected the interpretation of medieval Jerusalem itself, as it became first a Christian and then a Muslim city. By the same process, the Israelite Temple of

The women with Joseph of Arimathea "came to the tomb, taking the spices that they had prepared ... but when they went in, they did not find the body" (Luke 24:3). Two of the women depicted on the facade of the tomb of Jesus in Bologna carry small unguent jars for anointing the body; the third points toward an accompanying relief showing an angel seated on an empty sarcophagus. According to the Gospel of Mark, when the women entered the tomb, a young man in a white robe, sitting on the right side of the tomb, reassured them: "Do not be alarmed; you are looking for Jesus of Nazareth, who was crucified. He has been raised. He is not here" (Mark 16:6).

Jerusalem became associated with the Church of the Holy Sepulchre.[22] Medieval pilgrims to the Holy Sepulchre saw there not only relics of Christendom, but the relic of the horn with which David was anointed, the ring with which Solomon sealed the demons (according to legend, to control them, so that they would build the Temple for him), the altar of Abraham on Mount Moriah, the tomb of Adam, and the site of the martyrdom of the high priest Zechariah—all associated with the destroyed Jewish Temple. The Holy Sepulchre became, in Eusebius's words, "the New Jerusalem, facing the far-famed Jerusalem of old time."[23] Set opposite the ruins of the old Temple, Constantine's new church was from its inception symbolically transformed into the new Temple. Thus even the sacred geography of Jerusalem itself was flexible.

The church's rich associations faced some competition when the Dome of Rock was built on the Temple platform at the end of the seventh century, following the Muslim conquest of Jerusalem.[24] Located on or near the site of the original Israelite Temple, the Dome of the Rock attains much of its symbolic meaning from a combination of its historical associations with the Jewish Temple and its formal relationship with the Holy Sepulchre and other Christian buildings. Its octagonal plan follows that of an early Christian martyrium (martyr's shrine), and its dome has precisely the same diameter as the Anastasis Rotunda of the Holy Sepulchre. As a consequence, several levels of meanings bind the two sites. It is no wonder the Crusaders were a bit confused when they conquered Jerusalem in 1099 as to what exactly the Dome of the Rock represented—for them it was simultaneously the Jewish Temple, a Muslim commemorative building and a Christian church.[25]

The idea of the relationship between copy and prototype can also inform our view of the present building of the Holy Sepulchre in Jerusalem, as the damaged historic stones of the building are being systematically replaced with newly fabricated copies. This contrasts with the Middle Ages, when there was a reverence (or at least a sense of obligation) toward the older components—a reverence that ultimately outweighed aesthetic and even structural concerns during the various rebuildings. In each successive reconstruction, the old stones were reused—not as a matter of economy, but because the ancient masonry had assumed religious significance. By its very antiquity, the building itself had come to be regarded as a relic. In fact, the combination of the old and the new, and the occasionally jarring contrast between them, was perhaps the most remarkable and most evocative aspect of the medieval phases of the Holy Sepulchre. The new architecture could, in effect, frame the old and add to its luster.

Sadly, with the heavy-handed reconstructions of the last decades, many of the old stones have disappeared, replaced by pristine replicas. Much of this was necessary, of course, with the cracking and deterioration of the masonry from the fires of the 19th century. Still, as copies have replaced their prototypes *in situ*, the relationship between the older and newer components in the building has been altered; the new no longer frames the old in quite the same way. Instead we are left with an archaeological puzzle, as we attempt to determine what is originally from the 2nd, 4th, 11th or 12th century, and what from each period was replaced in the restorations of the 19th and 20th centuries.

For the purist, for whom old stones still mean something— either archaeologically or religiously—one can still find souvenirs of the Holy Sepulchre elsewhere in Jerusalem. That is to say, if you go to Jerusalem, don't look for all the stones of the Holy Sepulchre at the Holy Sepulchre. For just as the relics of the Holy Sepulchre were disseminated around Europe by pilgrims during the Middle Ages, so too the damaged stones of the building have been dispersed throughout Jerusalem by modern restoration architects. A few capitals may be seen at the entrance of the Greek Orthodox Patriarchate. Others are in the courtyard of the Museum of the Flagellation, including the monogrammed Byzantine capitals from the 11th-century rotunda. Still others, including the original column shafts and capitals from the early Christian Anastasis Rotunda, now decorate the garden in the Church of All Nations.

During the Middle Ages, images and objects traveled as the bearers of meaning—ideas that had been made palpable and concrete in physical form. Whether as descriptions or as a miniature image on a flask carried home by a pilgrim or even as a piece of real estate said to have been transported by angels (like the Holy House of Loreto in Italy, which had been brought from Nazareth), a sort of topographical transfer occurred. The myriad spiritual associations of one location could be made mystically present in a new setting. The symbolic replication of sacred objects and sites led to the creation of new centers of veneration for pilgrims. The topography of Jerusalem was transported in a variety of ways—even within Jerusalem itself—so that the faithful could be spiritually transported to the New Jerusalem.

Notes

1. Much of this article derives from Robert Ousterhout, "Flexible Geography and Transportable Topography," in *The Real and Ideal Jerusalem in Jewish, Christian, and Islamic Art*, ed. Bianca Kuehnel, *Jewish Art* 23-24 (1997-1998), pp. 393-404.

2. See Gabriel Barkay, "The Garden Tomb—Was Jesus Buried Here?" *Biblical Archaeology Review* March/April 1986; and Jerome Murphy-O'Connor, "The Garden Tomb and the Misfortunes of an Inscription," *Biblical Archaeology Review*, March/April 1986.

3. Jerome Murphy-O'Connor, *The Holy Land* (Oxford: Oxford Univ. Press, 1998), p. 141.

4. Eusebius, *Life of Constantine* 3.40, in *Egeria's Travels to the Holy Land*, trans. John Wilkinson (Warminster, UK: Aris & Phillips, 1981), p. 171.

5. Michael Avi-Yonah, *The Madaba Mosaic Map* (Jerusalem: Israel Exploration Society, 1954); and more recently, Michelle Piccirillo and Eugenio Alliata, eds., *The Madaba Map Centenary* (Jerusalem: Franciscan Printing Press, 1999).

6. Virgilio C. Corbo, *Il Santo Sepolcro de Gerusalemme* (Jerusalem, 1981), 3 vols.

7. For a summary of the history, see Robert Ousterhout, "Rebuilding the Temple: Constantine Monomachus and the Holy Sepulchre," *Journal of the Society of Architectural Historians* 48 (1989), pp. 66-78. More recently, see Joan Taylor and Shimon Gibson, *Beneath the Church of the Holy Sepulchre* (London: Palestine Exploration Fund, 1994), for important observations on the site of the Constantinian building; their suggestions for its reconstruction are less useful. See also Martin Biddle, *The Tomb of Christ* (Sutton, 1999), whose suggestions for redating both the 11th- and 12th-century phases of construction have not been generally accepted.

8. Eusebius, *Life of Constantine* 3.26-27, in Wilkinson, *Egeria's Travels*, pp. 164-165.

9. Corbo, *Santo Sepolcro, passim.*

10. Ousterhout, "Rebuilding the Temple," *passim.*

11. For a recent analysis of the Crusader building, see Jaroslav Folda, *The Art of the Crusaders in the Holy Land, 1098-1187* (Cambridge and New York: Cambridge Univ. Press, 1995), pp. 175-245, with its important observations on the chronology of construction, the majority of which he places in the decade 1040-1049.

12. Robert Venturi, *Complexity and Contradiction in Architecture* (New York: Museum of Modern Art, 1966).

13. See Ousterhout, "The Church of S. Stefano: A 'Jerusalem' in Bologna," *Gesta* 20 (1981), pp. 311-321; also Gina Fasoli, ed., *Stefaniana: Contributi per la storia del complesso di S. Stefano in Bologna*, Deputazione di Storia Patria per le Provincie de Romagna, Documenti e studi 17 (Bologna, 1985).

14. A. Testi Rasponi, "Note marginale al Liber Pontificalis di Agnello," *R. Deputazione di Storia Patria per le Provincie di Romagna, Atti e memorie* 4:2 (1912), pp. 202-203.

15. Gary Vikan, *Byzantine Pilgrimage Art* (Washington, DC: Dumbarton Oaks, 1982); Ousterhout, ed., *The Blessings of Pilgrimage* (Urbana, IL: Univ. of Illinois Press, 1990).

16. Charles Rufus Morey, "The Painted Panel from the Sancta Sanctorum," *Festschrift zum sechzigsten Geburtstag von Paul Clemen* (Bonn-Dusseldorf: F. Cohen, 1926), p. 150ff.; Vikan, *Byzantine Pilgrimage Art*, pp. 18-20.

17 See the seminal discussion by Richard Krautheimer, "Introduction to an 'Iconography of Medieval Architecture,'" *Journal of the Warburg and Courtauld Institutes* 5 (1942), pp. 1-33, reprinted in Krautheimer, *Studies in Early Christian, Medieval, and Renaissance Art* (New York: New York Univ. Press, 1969), pp. 115-150; also see Ousterhout, "Loca Sancta and the Architectural Response to Pilgrimage," in *Blessings of Pilgrimage*, pp. 108-124.

18. J. Hubert, "Le Saint-Sepulcre de Neuvy et les pelerinages de Terre Sainte au XIe siècle," *Bulletin monumental* 90 (1931), pp. 91-100.

19. Friedrich Oswald, Leo Schaefer and Hans Rudolf Sennhauser, *Vorromanische Kirchenbauten* (Munich: Prestel, 1971), pp. 87-89; Ousterhout, "Loca Sancta," p. 114.

20. Karl Young, *The Dramatic Associations of the Easter Sepulchre* (Madison: Univ. of Wisconsin Press, 1920), pp. 93-94.

21. Ousterhout, "Flexible Geography," pp. 399-402.

22. Ousterhout, "The Temple, the Sepulchre, and the Martyrion of the Savior," *Gesta* 39 (1990), pp. 44-53.

23. Eusebius, *Life of Constantine* 3.33, in Wilkinson, *Egeria's Travels*, p. 167.

24. Oleg Grabar, *The Formation of Islamic Art* (New Haven: Yale Univ Press, 1973), pp. 64-65.

25. Daniel Weiss, "Hec est Domus Domini Firmiter Edificata: The Image of the Temple in Crusader Art," in Kuehnel, *Real and Ideal Jerusalem*, pp. 210-217.

CHAPTER 6

⚜

A Smithy in a Crusader Church

DAN BAHAT

Because my interest in the archaeology of Jerusalem is well known about the city, local residents often come to me with questions, finds and ideas. That is how I came upon an unknown Crusader church some 20 years ago.

Someone suggested that I examine a blacksmith shop in the Muslim Quarter of the Old City. I've never been reluctant to go on these excursions because I know from experience that there is much I can learn from such "archaeological" tips.

The street where the blacksmith shop was located is known as Aqabat Haladiyah; it is in the northeastern quadrant of the Old City, west of the Temple Mount. When we arrived at the smithy, we were welcomed by the two brothers who owned the workshop, Nagi and Rafiq Baslamit. They courteously gave us permission to examine the structure in which they were busily shoeing donkeys, which are used to make deliveries of heavy goods in the winding streets of the Old City.

The workshop had an east-west orientation. It was divided almost in thirds by two rows of three pillars running east-west. On the perimeter wall, engaged pillars (pilasters) were placed opposite each of the free-standing pillars. The twelve bays—four in the central nave and four each in the side aisles—were roofed with cross vaults created by handsome ribbing. Around the walls and the engaged pillars extended a so-called running cornice. On the eastern wall, we saw two semi-circular apses, the center one slightly larger than the one beside it. A similar apse on the other side of the slightly larger center apse was no longer extant.

These architectural elements left no doubt in my mind that this blacksmith workshop was housed in a Crusader church built in the form of a basilica—probably dating from the 12th century. The orientation of the apses to the east (as in almost all early churches), the running cornice and the vaulted roof were unmistakable signs of Crusader construction.

Our initial efforts to identify the church failed. A full description of the street on which the smithy was located is given by Père Vincent and Père Abel in their classic description of Jerusalem, *Jerusalem Nouvelle* (1926), but they make no mention of this building. We next went to scholarly maps showing Crusader Jerusalem, but were surprised to find that the maps left this section of the city almost empty; not one map indicated that a church had stood on the site of our blacksmith shop.

Could it be that here was an existing Crusader church that had completely escaped notice both in ancient and modern sources?

We decided that a thorough survey of the building was needed. The owners of the building were delighted that they were working in such a distinguished structure, and they were happy to cooperate.

The church is neither large nor small as Crusader churches go. The center nave is about 13 feet wide and the two side aisles are each about 10.5 feet wide. The church is 48 feet long. The two extant apses are not precise semi-circles because they are wider than they are deep. Only the center apse protrudes on the outside of the building; it is contained in a rectangular chevet (the apsidal termination of the east end of a church). The smaller side apses are built into the eastern wall and do not protrude on the outside of the building. Original lancet windows (high, narrow, sharply arched windows) are in the center and the northern apses (the southern apse was reconstructed in a later phase). The center apse has, in addition to the windows, two niches. Similar niches have been noted in another Crusader church, but we have no idea what they were used for.

Our detailed survey of the building also revealed that the

church had undergone three phases of construction. The finest work was done in the original phase. In the second phase, the northern and western walls were apparently reconstructed; the quality of the new masonry and the running cornice is greatly inferior to that of the original phase, as can be seen where the running cornice of the second phase joins the running cornice of the original phase. In the third and last phase, the southern aisle (including the southern apse) was rebuilt. This work was also crudely done and the only barrel vault (in the southwest bay) belongs to this third phase.

Unfortunately, we were unable to examine the floor of the church. At present the church is only about 19 feet high. The owners of the workshop claim that some years ago the floor was about six feet lower than at present, but that is the only information we have. So it is impossible even to estimate how far below the present floor the original floor of the church lies.

In our continuing efforts to identify our church in ancient sources, we have come across an ancient deed (dated January 1177) for the sale of a house in Jerusalem that was built against the Capitium of the Church of St. Julien. This Church of St. Julien has never been identified. From what we know about the location of this house, it appears that our blacksmith shop may well have been the Church of St. Julien mentioned in this deed, although the identification is by no means certain.

⛭

CHAPTER 7

Church of the Apostles Found on Mt. Zion

BARGIL PIXNER

After the Crusaders conquered Jerusalem in 1099, they identified the remains of a church on the city's southwestern hill (today called Mt. Zion) as the site of the tomb of King David. Even more important to them, however, local tradition associated the site with important events from the time of Jesus: the Last Supper, appearances of the resurrected Christ, the descent of the Holy Spirit upon the apostles on Pentecost, and the dormition (passing away) of Mary.

Then the Crusaders did what Crusaders often did with holy sites: They rebuilt it as a church and memorial.

At least since Crusader times, this site has been venerated as the place where David was laid to rest; and the second floor of the structure has been revered as the so-called cenacle—the "upper room" (see Mark 14:15; Luke 22:12; Acts 1:13) of the Last Supper.

The Crusaders were right in identifying this site as an ancient holy precinct. In fact, it is almost certainly the site of the Church of the Apostles, which supposedly marked the place where the apostles prayed after witnessing the resurrected Christ lifted into heaven on the Mount of Olives (Acts 1:1-13).

But archaeology presents a somewhat more complicated picture, which I will sketch in by making three principal arguments: (1) This site on Mt. Zion is not the site of the tomb of David but of a Roman-period synagogue (all scholars agree on this point);

(2) the synagogue was not a usual Jewish synagogue but a Judeo-Christian synagogue; and (3) this Judeo-Christian synagogue only later became known as the Church of the Apostles.

The Bible tells us that King David captured Metsudat Tsion (2 Samuel 5:7), the Fortress of Zion, which became the City of David. According to 1 Kings 2:10, David was later "buried in the city of David." Although ancient Israelite burials almost always occurred outside the city so as not to contaminate the city with the impurity associated with a dead body, an exception was made for the royal line from David to Ahaz.[1]

The traditional (though not actual) tomb of David was located on Mount Zion (Zion III), Jerusalem's high southwestern hill, just inside (left of) the curve in the road in the lower half of this photo. On the summit of Mount Zion is the Church of the Dormition, with its conical roof and four corner towers, which housed the traditional site of David's tomb and a late-first-century A.D. Judeo-Christian synagogue, later called the Church of the Apostles. To the east (right) is Jerusalem's narrower southeastern hill, the City of David (Zion I), which extends south from the Temple Mount (Zion II).

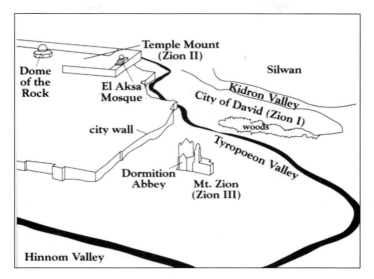

The site now known as Mt. Zion is a broad hill south of the walled Old City. In fact, two hills lie south of the Old City: a western hill, the modern Mt. Zion; and a lower, narrower, steeply sloped eastern hill.

Until a little over a century ago, scholars generally agreed that the City of David lay on the western hill. So there was no reason to question the traditional site of David's tomb on (the modern) Mt. Zion. Then, in 1838, the American orientalist Edward Robinson crawled through a fantastic tunnel under the eastern hill that carried water from one side of the hill to the other. What was this tunnel doing under the eastern hill? In 1880, an ancient Hebrew inscription found on the wall of this tunnel helped the German architect Conrad Schick to identify the tunnel as the one constructed by the Israelite king Hezekiah (727-698 B.C.) to bring water into Jerusalem, in anticipation of an Assyrian siege (see 2 Kings 18:13-19:37; 2 Chronicles 32).

The question remained: What was all this doing under the eastern hill? A subsequent century of excavation has now conclusively established that the Canaanite (or Jebusite) city that David captured in about 1000 B.C. and that then became known as the City of David (2 Samuel 5:7) was on the eastern hill, not on the western hill. This was the original Mt. Zion (Zion I).

This is the author's tentative reconstruction of the first-century Judeo-Christian synagogue that later became known as the Church of the Apostles. The shaded stones represent extant remains.

King Solomon, David's son, built his palace and a Temple to the Lord on a hill north of the City of David (on the eastern hill). This northern hill is today still called the Temple Mount, with the Dome of the Rock at its center. Sometime after Solomon's building projects on the northern hill were completed, this hill became known as Mt. Zion (Zion II). This shift to the Temple Mount is already noticeable in Isaiah (for example, Isaiah 60:14) and in the Psalms, but is especially clear in the First Book of Maccabees (4:37,60, 5:54, 7:33).

The Temple Mount remained Mt. Zion (Zion II) until the Romans destroyed Jerusalem (along with the Temple) in 70 A.D. With the city in ruins, late-first-century residents of Jerusalem could not imagine that the splendid palace of David once stood on the lowly eastern hill; rather, it must have stood on the city's highest hill, the western hill. The late-first-century Jewish historian Josephus refers to the western hill as the City of David.[2] Thus the western hill became the third Mt. Zion (Zion III), a name it retains (erroneously) to this day.

By the tenth century, Christian tradition placed David's tomb on the western hill (Zion III), which had long been identified as Mt. Zion. The first known reference to the location of David's tomb on the western hill comes in a very confused document called *"The Life of Saint Helene and Constantine,"* written in the tenth century by an unidentified Greek author to eulogize the work of Emperor Constantine's mother, Helena.[3]

Once the Crusaders arrived in Jerusalem, they found that a Byzantine church called Hagia Sion (Holy Zion) on today's Mt. Zion (Zion III) had been destroyed. In a better-preserved annex south of the church, they discovered what had been identified as David's tomb and the tombs of Solomon and St. Stephen. The latter tombs were attached to David's tomb.[4]

The Crusaders disregarded the tradition concerning Stephen's tomb, because a Byzantine Church of St. Stephen containing a reliquary of the martyr already existed north of Jerusalem's Damascus Gate (it's still there, on the grounds of the École Biblique). But the Crusaders marked David's tomb with an enormous Gothic cenotaph (an empty sarcophagus).

For the Crusaders, however, David's tomb was less important than another tradition, that this sanctuary was a site associated with Jesus' crucifixion and resurrection, especially the Last Supper.

The Crusaders' identification of David's tomb on Mt. Zion (Zion III) was gradually accepted by Muslims and Jews. (This was especially important for Jews from 1948 to 1967, when the Old City was in Jordanian hands, because the most-revered Jewish site, the Wailing Wall—the western wall of Herod's Temple Mount, inside the Old City—was largely inaccessible to Jews but Mt. Zion was under Israeli control.) In 1948, during Israel's War of Independence, considerable fighting

After the Romans destroyed Jerusalem in 70 A.D., a group of Judeo-Christians built a synagogue using fallen ashlars (the large shaped stones of the wall) from the ruins of Herodian buildings, perhaps even of the Temple itself. It is possible that these early Christians deliberately used stones from the destroyed Temple to transfer the holiness of the Jewish site to their new church-synagogue.

HERSHEL SHANKS

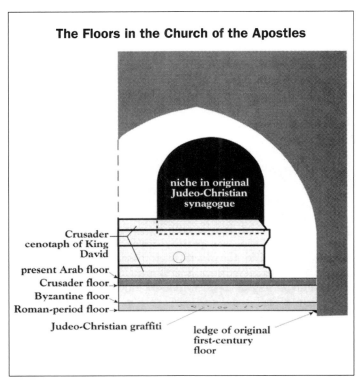

The Floors in the Church of the Apostles

niche in original Judeo-Christian synagogue

Crusader cenotaph of King David

present Arab floor
Crusader floor
Byzantine floor
Roman-period floor

Judeo-Christian graffiti

ledge of original first-century floor

In the early 1950s Israeli archaeologist Jacob Pinkerfeld removed the present marble floor and dug two pits that revealed three earlier floors. Five inches below the present floor was a 12th-century Crusader floor; 1.5 feet below that was a mosaic floor with geometric designs dating to the fifth century; 4 inches below the mosaic were remains of a Roman floor (late first century A.D.) consisting of plaster fragments and stones. A foundation ledge projecting into the hall at this level indicated that it was the original building's floor.

occurred on and around Mt. Zion, in the course of which a shell exploded in the building housing the traditional tomb of King David. In 1951 the Israeli archaeologist Jacob Pinkerfeld was entrusted to repair the damage. While doing so, he also examined the site from an archaeological perspective.[5]

Behind the cenotaph of King David, Pinkerfeld found a niche that was part of the original structure of the building. When he removed the marble floor slabs for repair, he dug two trial pits in which he found three earlier floor levels. About 5 inches below the present floor, he found the Crusader floor. About a foot and a half below that he found a late-Roman or early-Byzantine floor with colored mosaic with geometric designs. Then, about 4 inches below that, Pinkerfeld found the plaster of the original building's floor, along with the remains of what appeared to be a stone pavement.

In Pinkerfeld's excavation report he described this original floor:

> Seventy cm below the present floor level another floor of plaster was found, quite possibly the remains of a stone pavement. Some small fragments of smooth stones, perhaps the remains of this pavement, were found slightly above the level ... It is certain that this floor belonged to the original building, i.e., to the period when the northern wall and its apse [niche] were built. This is evident from a section of the wall which shows at that level a foundation ledge projecting into the hall.[6]

As Pinkerfeld noted, in the northern wall (which was part of the original construction) was a niche about 6 feet above the original floor level. Similar niches at similar heights above floor level have been found in ancient synagogues and were presumably used to house an ark for Torah scrolls. Pinkerfeld reasoned that this niche served the same function. He concluded that the building was originally a Roman-period synagogue.

That this building was originally a synagogue now seems clear, and scholars who have examined the matter agree. The next step is to determine what kind of synagogue it was. Was it a traditional Jewish synagogue, or a Judeo-Christian synagogue?

The earliest Christians were Jews who did not regard themselves as having abandoned Judaism. Indeed, one of the earliest questions that the new religion addressed was whether gentiles—non-Jews—could become Christians or whether it was necessary to be a Jew in order to become a Christian (see Acts 15). Moreover, for several centuries Judeo-Christians and even some gentile Christians referred to their houses of worship as synagogues.[7] In Hebrew the Jewish house of prayer was—and still is—called Beit (or Beth) Knesset, which means simply "house of assembly."

Under Hellenistic influence, this became "synagogue," a Greek word meaning "assembly."

To distinguish themselves from Jews, gentile Christians began to refer to their gatherings by the Greek word *ekklesia*, also meaning "assembly." This word was then applied to the gathering place and later to the church building itself. Another word for the building was the Greek *kyriake* ("belonging to the Lord"), from which the English word "church" is derived.

Pinkerfeld concluded that the original structure on Mt. Zion had been a Jewish synagogue, because, he thought, it was oriented precisely toward the Temple Mount, whereas churches are usually oriented toward the east.[8]

In fact, however, Christian houses of worship did not become oriented to the east until the second half of the fourth century, after Christianity had become the official religion of Rome. The construction that concerns us here is of a much earlier date. Also, this synagogue—or more precisely, its niche—is not oriented exactly toward the Temple Mount, where the Jewish Temple once stood. Rather, it is oriented slightly off north, toward the Church of the Holy Sepulchre, which, at the time the synagogue was built, was believed to be the site of Jesus' tomb and crucifixion.

Was this orientation intentional? I believe it was. Would it not be logical for Judeo-Christians to orient their synagogues toward the new center of their redemption? In 326 A.D. this is exactly how the emperor Constantine oriented the Church of the Martyrion,[9] the earliest section of the Church of the Holy Sepulchre—toward Jesus' tomb.

But there is more. In the lowest layer of the Mt. Zion structure, Pinkerfeld found pieces of plaster with Greek graffiti scratched on them that came from the original synagogue wall.[10] These graffiti were ultimately published by a team of experts from the Studium Biblicum Franciscanum led by Professors Emmanuele Testa and Bellarmino Bagatti. One graffito has the words "Conquer, Savior, mercy"; another translates as "O Jesus, that I may live, O Lord of the autocrat [King David?]."[11] This was clearly a Christian, or Judeo-Christian, place of worship.

The historical conditions after the Roman destruction of Jerusalem in 70 A.D. and some new archaeological evidence suggest the circumstances under which this Judeo-Christian synagogue was built.

In 70 A.D. the Roman general Titus suppressed the First Jewish Revolt (66-70 A.D.) by utterly destroying Jerusalem and burning the Temple. The first-century historian Josephus tells us that the destruction reached the farthest corners of the city and was so complete that passers-by would not know a city ever stood there.[12]

This destruction included the western hill, Mt. Zion (Zion III). In 1983, during an excavation in the Dormition Abbey, the building on Mt. Zion adjacent to this ancient Judeo-Christian synagogue, I found coins dating from the second and third years of the First Jewish Revolt (67 and 68 A.D.) on the steps of a ritual bath lying under huge layers of destruction debris, and in the remains of an oven. Thus it is safe to conclude that the building that stood on the site of the adjacent Judeo-Christian synagogue also fell victim to the Roman onslaught.

The Judeo-Christian community in Jerusalem escaped this terrible catastrophe by fleeing to Pella in Transjordan and the countryside of Gilean and Bashan[13] in expectation of the *Parousia*, the second coming of Christ.[14]

When this did not occur and they realized that the time of Jesus' return was not yet at hand, they decided to go back to Jerusalem to rebuild their sanctuary on the site of the ancient "upper room"—where the Last Supper had been held, where the apostles returned after witnessing Jesus' ascension on the Mount of Olives and where Peter delivered his Pentecost sermon as recorded in Acts 2. It was on this site that they built their synagogue. They were free to do so because they enjoyed a certain religious freedom from the Romans (*religio licita*) in that they were Jews who confessed Jesus as their Messiah, and not gentile converts. (Roman law recognized as legitimate the religion practiced by Jews, even worship of Jesus; gentiles who became Christians, however, were persecuted until the time of Constantine.)

The archaeological evidence is consistent with this suggestion. On the outside face of the synagogue, at the base of the eastern and southern walls, we can see building stones of the original

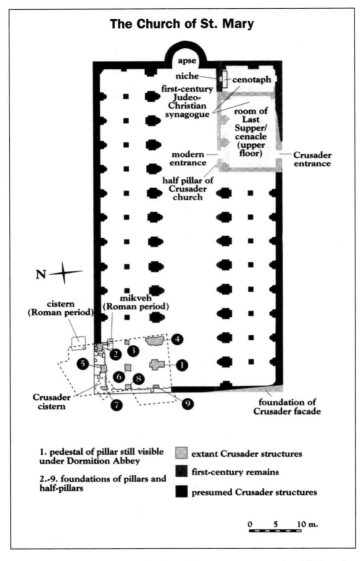

The Church of St. Mary

apse

niche — cenotaph

first-century Judeo-Christian synagogue

room of Last Supper/ cenacle (upper floor)

modern entrance

half pillar of Crusader church

Crusader entrance

N

mikveh (Roman period)

cistern (Roman period)

Crusader cistern

foundation of Crusader facade

1. pedestal of pillar still visible under Dormition Abbey

2.-9. foundations of pillars and half-pillars

extant Crusader structures

first-century remains

presumed Crusader structures

0   5   10 m.

Roman-period building, which still exists to a considerable height. These stones, however, date to the Herodian period, that is, before the 70 A.D. destruction of the Temple. The synagogue's stones, then, were not originally hewn for this building but were brought from elsewhere.

Thus, in the late first century, Judeo-Christians returning to Jerusalem built this synagogue by re-using stones already cut for another purpose (probably a building abandoned or destroyed during the First Revolt). They put up their synagogue on the site they—and the Crusaders long after them—identified with the cenacle (the "upper room" where the Last Supper was held) and associated with the early Judeo-Christian community led by James, "the brother of the Lord" (Galatians 1:19).

The building was probably constructed between 70 and 132 A.D. According to Eusebius, during those years there was a flourishing Judeo-Christian community in Jerusalem presided over by a series of 13 bishops from the circumcision (that is, Judeo-Christians).[15] Early Church writers identified this Judeo-Christian synagogue as the Church of the Apostles.

Why was this ancient Judeo-Christian synagogue on Mt. Zion (Zion III) called the Church of the Apostles?

According to Bishop Epiphanius (315-403 A.D.), when the Roman emperor Hadrian visited Jerusalem in 130/131 A.D., there was standing on Mt. Zion "a small church of God. It marked the site of the *Hypero-on* [upper room] to which the disciples returned from the Mount of Olives after the Lord had been taken up. It had been built on that part of Sion."[16] This "small church" could only have been a Judeo-Christian synagogue.

Another source, a Patriarch of Alexandria named Euthychius (896-940 A.D.), tells us that the Judeo-Christians who fled to Pella to escape the Roman destruction of Jerusalem in 70 A.D. "returned to Jerusalem in the fourth year of the emperor

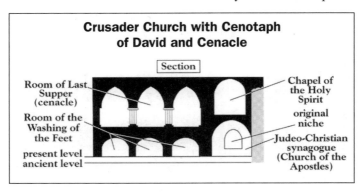

Crusader Church with Cenotaph of David and Cenacle

Section

Room of Last Supper (cenacle)

Room of the Washing of the Feet

present level
ancient level

Chapel of the Holy Spirit

original niche

Judeo-Christian synagogue (Church of the Apostles)

Vespasian [73 A.D.], and built there their church."[17] The Judeo-Christians returned to Jerusalem under the leadership of Simon Bar-Kleopha, who was the second bishop of Jerusalem after James, "the brother of the Lord," and, like Jesus, a descendant of the royal Davidic family.

This suggests an intriguing possibility—that the stones in secondary use in the synagogue were taken from the Temple itself, standing on Zion II, with the intention of transferring some elements of the ancient Holy Temple to the site of a new Mt. Zion.

From this time on, the western hill of Jerusalem was referred to by Christians as Mt. Zion (Zion III). In the fifth century, the French politician and historian Eucherius mentioned the church on Mt. Zion:

> The plain upper part [of Mt. Zion] is occupied by monks' cells, which surround a church. Its foundations, it is said, have been laid by the Apostles in reverence to the place of the resurrection of the Lord. It was there that they were filled with the Spirit of the Paraclete [the Holy Spirit] as promised by the Lord.[18]

In saying that the foundations were "laid by the Apostles in reverence to the place of the resurrection of the Lord," Eucherius may have meant that the building was oriented toward Jesus' tomb in the Holy Sepulchre Church, which was also the site of the resurrection.

In 348 A.D., just a few decades after the Roman emperor Constantine declared Christianity a legal religion, a priest named Cyril, who later became bishop of Jerusalem, delivered a famous sermon in the newly constructed basilica of the Holy Sepulchre. In his address, he said it would have been more appropriate to speak about the Holy Spirit in the very place where the Pentecost Spirit descended upon the apostles—namely "in the Upper Church of the Apostles."[19]

The construction of the first Byzantine church on Mt. Zion was ordered by Theodosius I, who reigned between 379 and 395 A.D. The structure of the apostolic synagogue was left untouched, however. The new church simply formed a kind of vestibule to the ancient structure. This we know from the famous mosaic in the apse of the Pudentiana church in Rome, which was made about 400 A.D. This mosaic not only shows the Church of the Holy Sepulchre but also the two buildings on Mt. Zion next to each other.

From the textual evidence, it appears that the Byzantine vestibule church, adjacent to the Church of the Apostles, was built as an octagon. The octagonal form was used for Christian memorial churches, in this case a memorial to the "mother of all churches," the Church of the Apostles.

To enhance the attraction of the Theodosian building, the presumed column of the flagellation of Jesus, which so far had been lying in the ruins of the house of Caiaphas, was inserted into the portico.[20] Crowds of people came to venerate this column on Good Friday morning, according to Egeria, a female pilgrim who visited Jerusalem around 394 A.D. From her description of the liturgy, there was a double sanctuary on Mt. Zion,[21] the old Church of the Apostles and the Theodosian Church in front of it.

On Pentecost, it appears, the laity gathered in the newly built church of Theodosius, while the presbyters (ordained priests) convened in the ancient Judeo-Christian synagogue. In a passage in the dedication sermon of Bishop John II of Jerusalem (387-419), the builders, priests and architects are exhorted to go to the "upper room."

The Church of Hagia Sion was burnt during the Persian invasion of 614 A.D. It was rebuilt by Patriarch Modestos, and partially destroyed again in 1009 A.D. by Hakim, the Fatimid sultan of Egypt.

When the Crusaders arrived in Jerusalem at the end of the 11th century, they found the Byzantine Church of Hagia Sion in ruins. On the south part of the ruins of the Hagia Sion, the Crusaders built a new church, which they named St. Mary of Mt. Zion, in memory of the tradition that Mary had lived on Mt. Zion after the resurrection of her soul and had also died there.

In 1985, while a sewage channel was being dug in front of the Dormition Abbey, I took the occasion to examine the area archaeologically and was able to locate the foundation of the facade of this Crusader church. The southwest corner of the church is in exact alignment with the southern wall of the ancient Judeo-Christian synagogue. The bases of nine Crusader pilasters and the western section of the northern wall of the Crusader church were also discovered and preserved.

Thus it was the Crusaders who first included the walls of the ancient Judeo-Christian synagogue, which had become the Church of the Apostles, into their own basilica.

Above the remaining walls of the Church of the Apostles, the Crusaders built a second floor, which may have been the actual site of the "upper room." This room is still visited today by Christian pilgrims. On the lower floor, next to the pseudo-tomb of David, the Crusaders commemorated the place where Christ washed the feet of his disciples (John 13:1-20).

When the Crusaders were forced to leave Jerusalem after their defeat at the Horns of Hattin near Tiberias in 1187 A.D., they entrusted their church on Mt. Zion to Syrian Christians.[22] The entire complex on Mt. Zion was destroyed by order of one of the Ayyubid sultans of Damascus just a few decades later (1219 A.D.). Christian pilgrims of the 13th and early 14th centuries lament in their journals that the Church of the Apostles and the cenacle are in a state of disrepair.[23]

Near the end of the Crusader period, a travel account written in Hebrew by a Spanish Jew named Benjamin of Tudela (1167 A.D.) directs us to the "Tomb of David" on Mt. Zion. Benjamin relates that during his stay in Jerusalem, a Jew named Abraham told him a fantastic story. While employed by the Christian patriarch to reconstruct a damaged monument on Mt. Zion, two Jewish workers accidentally happened upon a secret passage and suddenly found themselves in a palace made of marble columns—the tombs of David and the Kings of Israel! A golden scepter and golden crown rested upon a table. There were riches all around. Suddenly they were struck down by a fierce whirlwind and began to hear voices telling them to leave immediately. Frightened, they crept back through the secret passageway, out into the open.

They related their discovery to the patriarch. The patriarch with the help of Abraham, wrote a report to Constantinople. After three days, the two workmen were found sick in bed. They could not be persuaded to return to the site. They reported: "We shall never again return there, for God does not want this place to be seen by any human being."[24]

As fantastic and confused as their story may sound, it became the basis of Jewish folklore concerning the tomb of David. Soon the local Muslims also accepted the site as authentic.

Between 1335 and 1337 A.D. the Franciscan fathers, who had recently arrived in the Holy Land, purchased the site on Mt. Zion from the Saracens. The king of Naples served as an intermediary in this affair. Thus Mt. Zion became the first convent of the Franciscans in the Holy Land. Since then the Franciscans have been entrusted with the care of the holy places. To this day the Superior of the Franciscans carries the title *Custos Sancti Montis Sion*, "Custodian of Holy Mt. Zion."

The Franciscan friars repaired the roof of the cenacle ("upper room") in the 14th century, strengthening it with a gothic rib vaulting. South of the cenacle they built their new monastery (Mt. Zion Monastery), which can still be seen today.

Apparently the Franciscans were never able to occupy the tomb of David on the ground floor, however. There Muslim holy men had made their abode. Indeed, local Muslims pleaded with the authorities to remove the infidels from the upper floor of the tomb of Nabi Dawood (the prophet David). These pressures became even more intense during the Turkish period. By the middle of the 16th century, the Franciscans were violently forced to abandon Mt. Zion completely.

To hinder their return, both David's tomb and the cenacle were declared mosques. A prayer niche (*mihrab*) was inserted in the wall indicating the direction of prayer toward Mecca. It was exactly opposite the orientation of the niche of the first century Judeo-Christian synagogue-church, which pointed to the Holy Sepulchre.

Since 1948, Mt. Zion has been part of Israel. The government's Department of Religious Affairs now administers both floors of the building. The pseudo-tomb of David is used as a Jewish synagogue and the "upper room" is left open for Christian visitors. Unfortunately, the only archaeological exploration of this very important site was the cursory examination by Pinkerfeld. Perhaps one day it will be excavated more thoroughly. In the mean-

time, we may venerate it as Christendom's most ancient shrine:
The mother of all churches.

Notes

1. "And Solomon slept with his fathers and was buried in the City of David" (1 Kings 11:43). For later kings, see 1 Kings 14:31, 15:8,24, 22:50 (verse 51 in Hebrew); 2 Kings 12:21 (verse 22 in Hebrew), 14:20, 15:7,38, 16:20.

2. Josephus thought that the ancient wall (First wall) encompassing the western hill had been built by David and Solomon (*The Jewish War* 5.143).

3. Donato Baldi, *Enchiridion Locorum Sanctorum* (Jerusalem: Franciscan Printing Press, 1982; reprint of the 2nd edition of 1955), no. 754.

4. Raymund de Aguilers writes: "In that church are the following holies: the sepulchre of King David and of Solomon and the sepulchre of the proto-martyr Saint Stephen" (Baldi, *Enchiridion*, no. 757).

5. This report was only published posthumously, the author was killed in a terrorist attack on the 1956 Archaeological Convention at Ramat Rachel, south of Jerusalem.

6. Jacob Pinkerfeld, "'David's Tomb,' Notes on the History of the Building," *Bulletin of the Louis Rubinowitz Fund for the Exploration of Ancient Synagogues* 3 (Jerusalem: Hebrew Univ., 1960), pp. 41-43.

7. See for example, Ignatius of Antioch (Letter to Polycarp 4:2); Pastor of Hermas 43:9; Justin the Martyr (Dialog with the Jew Tryphon 63:5).

8. Pinkerfeld, "David's Tomb," p. 43.

9. The Greek word *martyrion* means that the church was standing as a "witness" of the death and resurrection of Jesus Christ.

10. Pinkerfeld, "David's Tomb," p. 43.

11. Bellarmino Bagatti, *The Church from the Circumcision* (Jerusalem: Franciscan Printing Press, 1971), p. 121.

12. Josephus, *The Jewish War* 7.3-4.

13. Eusebius, *Church History* 3.5, 2-3; Epiphanius, *Panarion* 29.7; 30.2, 7.

14. "Ascension of Isaiah 4" in James H. Charlesworth, ed., *The Old Testament Pseudepigrapha*, vol. 2 (Garden City, NY: Doubleday, 1985), pp. 161f.

15. In his own words: "And the history also contains the remark that there also was a very big church of Christ in Jerusalem, made up of Jews, until the time of the siege of Hadrian" (Eusebius, *Demonstratio Evangelica* 3.5, in *Patristic Evidence for Jewish-Christian Sects*, ed. A.F.J. Klijn and G.J. Reinink [Leiden, Neth.: E.J. Brill, 1973], p. 139). The list of bishops is to be found in Eusebius, *Church History* 4.5:1-4.

16. Baldi, *Enchiridion*, no. 733.

17. J.P. Miqne, ed., *Patrologia Latina* (Paris, 1844), vol. 3, p. 985.

18. Baldi, *Enchiridion*, no. 735.

19. Baldi, *Enchiridion*, no. 730.

20. Baldi, *Enchiridion*, no. 734.

21. Baldi, *Enchiridion*, no. 732.

22. Baldi, *Enchiridion*, no. 763.

23. The Syrian Christians transferred the traditions of Mt. Zion to the church of St. Mark near the Armenian quarter, which they venerate also as the cenacle.

24. Baldi, *Enchiridion*, no. 760.

CHAPTER 8

The Holy Grail

From Symbol to Relic

ERIC WARGO

Throughout the long history of Christianity, the Holy Grail has served primarily as a symbol. But in the Crusader period (and then again in modern times) the search for the actual relic from the Last Supper was transformed into a consuming passion.

In *The Holy Grail* (2004), British historian and literary scholar Richard Barber traces the history of the Holy Grail through its many manifestations, and shows how some sketchy biblical and apocryphal references became a medieval emblem of redemption.[1] According to Barber, the earliest evidence of interest in the cup of the Last Supper as a relic appears in a late-seventh-century A.D. account of a pilgrimage to Palestine by a Frankish bishop named Arculf. Having been shipwrecked on his return voyage, Arculf was invited to stay at the abbey of Iona, off the west coast of Scotland, where he regaled the local abbot, Adomnan, with tales of his journey. Adomnan later recorded the tales in a three-volume work, *De Locis Sanctis* (*Concerning the Holy Places*).

Of the Church of the Holy Sepulchre in Jerusalem, Adomnan writes:

> Between the basilica of Golgotha and the Martyrium, there is a chapel in which is the chalice of the Lord, which he himself blessed with his own hand and gave to the apostles when reclining with them at supper the day before he suffered. The chalice is silver, has the measure of a Gaul-

ish pint, and has two handles fashioned on either side ... After the Resurrection, the Lord drank from this same chalice, according to the supping with the apostles. The holy Arculf saw it, and through an opening of the perforated lid of the reliquary where it reposes, he touched it with his own hand which he had kissed.[2]

Unfortunately, there is no other historical mention of this silver chalice.

The term that has come to denote this wonderful object, "grail," first appears in the prose romance *Perceval* by the French writer Chrétien de Troyes. Left unfinished at the author's death in 1190, the story concerns a young would-be knight who visits the mysterious castle of the Fisher King, where he witnesses a strange procession in which a gem-encrusted gold dish, called a "grail," is used to carry a host (communion wafer) to an ailing old man. It is not identified as the *Holy* Grail or even specifically associated with the Last Supper, though at one point it is described as "such a Holy thing." Adhering too strictly to his first lesson in manners—don't ask unnecessary questions—Perceval fails to inquire about the objects he has seen; however, he is later told, first by a mysterious woman and then by an old hermit, that he should have asked. The procession Perceval witnesses also includes a boy carrying a lance that bleeds from its tip, which may well be a reference to the lance used by the centurion to pierce Jesus' side on the cross (John 19:34). If so, the grail of the tale may also have been intended as an artifact of the Passion; but since the author never finished his story, we have no way of knowing for certain.

At Antioch in 1099, during the First Crusade, the unexpected discovery of a spear believed to be the centurion's lance that pierced Jesus' side (and would later figure in the Holy Grail stories) boosted the morale of an outnumbered Frankish army enough to defeat the Turks besieging them. A supposed piece of the True Cross was repeatedly carried into battle by the Christian armies defending Jerusalem in the 12th century. And by the time of the medieval Grail romances, relics of the Holy Blood were already known at various sites around Europe.

HOCHSCHUL UND LANDESBIBLIOTHEK FULDA

Jesus' blood is collected in a chalice, in this miniature from a 12th-century illuminated Gospel from the abbey of Weingarten in southern Germany. In the early 13th-century work *The History of the Grail*, the poet Robert de Boron wrote that Joseph of Arimathea used the cup from the Last Supper to collect Jesus' blood after the Crucifixion. Although this idea is found in no prior text, the poet may have been influenced by an iconographic tradition of which this miniature is the earliest-known example.

No doubt the Grail stories, with their promise of mystery, challenge and salvation, helped inspire the search for relics. The late-12th-century historian William of Tyre tells of an emerald bowl found in a mosque in Caesarea (north of Tel Aviv in Israel) during the First Crusade and brought back to Genoa as booty. It was identified as the Grail in the late 13th century by Jacobus de Voragine in his *Chronicle of Genoa*, and his identification was no doubt based on the Grail romances. The vessel, called *Il Sacro Catino* (*The Sacred Bowl*), was taken to Paris after Napoleon conquered Italy at the end of the 18th century and was later returned broken, and it can still be seen in Genoa's cathedral. The vessel is made of green glass, not emerald, and it was probably made in the 11th century.

Another object, an agate chalice in the cathedral of Valencia, Spain, has also been connected to the Last Supper. According to medieval legend, Peter brought the vessel with him to Rome; it was later spirited away to Spain during a period of Christian per-

PHOTO (C) THE METROPOLITAN MUSEUM OF ART/THE CLOISTERS COLLECTION 1950 (50.4)

Jesus and the 12 disciples are depicted among the spreading branches of a vine in this elaborately gilded, 8-inch-high silver chalice, found near Antioch in 1910. Inside the chalice was an undecorated silver cup, which some early 20th-century scholars identified as the Holy Grail. Both the silver cup and its exquisite gilt silver container, however, have since been dated to the Byzantine period.

secution. The agate upper portion of the cup could date to the Roman period—there is no way to date it precisely—but its elaborately crafted mount is medieval.[3]

Grails have never stopped turning up—in archaeological sites, private collections and churches. Modern candidates for the holy cup include an elaborate silver Eucharist chalice or lamp found near Antioch in 1910 and currently in the Metropolitan Museum of Art in New York; identified in the 1930s as the Holy Grail, it has more recently been dated to the sixth century. One still-popular theory holds that the Holy Grail remains hidden somewhere in Scotland's Roslyn Chapel.

Modern writers have tended to turn the Holy Grail into a symbol for any sort of ideal or quest—whatever we feel will redeem or save us. One modern reinterpretation is that the Holy Grail, *san greal* in the original French, was really *sang real* or "royal blood." Redividing the French words in this way was originally suggested by a 15th-century English writer in reference to King Arthur, but the idea was revived and given a sensational, biblical twist in the 1982 bestseller *Holy Blood, Holy Grail*.[4] This book suggests that Jesus married Mary Magdalene and fathered a lineage of French kings—and that this secret bloodline was the real Holy Grail. Drawing heavily on this book as well as on Gnostic texts that seem to suggest a close or sexual relationship between Jesus and Mary Magdalene, Dan Brown's recent bestseller *The Da Vinci Code* has widely popularized the idea that the Holy Grail is a code word for the royal (or holy) bloodline of Jesus.[5] While these ideas make for exciting reading, there is nothing to substantiate them; stories of Jesus' physical affections for Mary are late and spurious.

As Richard Barber suggests, these fantastic ideas represent a perennial need to transform works of the imagination into something concrete—something that people hope may one day be found, like an actual physical cup (or plate, or chalice), or a long-buried scroll listing Jesus' descendants. The truth is something much harder to grasp and accept: The Holy Grail is a symbol, a metaphor and an idea that sprang from the fertile imaginations of medieval storytellers. You will find it digging in books, legends and myths, but not in the ground.

Notes

1. Richard Barber, *The Holy Grail* (Cambridge, MA: Harvard Univ. Press, 2004).

2. Quoted in Barber, *Holy Grail*, p. 167.

3. See Barber, *Holy Grail*, pp. 167-172.

4. Michael Baigent, Richard Leigh and Henry Lincoln, *Holy Blood, Holy Grail* (New York: Dell, 1982).

5. Dan Brown, *The Da Vinci Code* (New York: Doubleday, 2003).

Visiting Akko (Acre)

The Last Crusader City

WALTER ZANGER

O nce visited by St. Francis of Assisi, Marco Polo and thousands of Christian pilgrims on their way to Jerusalem, the
harbor of Akko was the last major outpost of the Crusaders in the
Holy Land. Today, the cavernous Crusader remains—now underground—are what attract most visitors. Before I venture into the
Crusader city, however, I always enjoy visiting the great mosque
of Ahmed Pasha, the 18th-century Ottoman governor of Akko,
whose violent ways earned him the nickname of el-Jazzar, "the
Butcher." With its sharply pointed minaret, arcaded courtyard
and numerous domes, the Akko mosque is the most Turkish-look-
ing building in Israel.

Just opposite the mosque is the entrance to the 12th- to 13th-
century Crusader city, which lies about 20 feet below the modern city. When the Arabs defeated the Crusaders for good in 1291,
they were determined to make the seacoast unusable. For the
Arabs, after all, no good came from the sea, only Crusaders! So
after throwing out the Christians, they destroyed as much of the
coastal cities as they could, in the case of Akko by burying its
important buildings and harbor facilities in rubble.

Today, only about 10 percent of the Crusader city (which they
called St. Jean d'Acre) has been dug out, but this part is very acces-
sible. Anyone who hasn't been to Akko recently will be astonished
by the buildings that have been uncovered. The castle built by the
crusading Order of St. John (called the Hospitallers because they

provided hospital and medical facilities to the Crusader population) stands right up against the northern walls of the city. One would think that the waterfront, to the south, would be a more desirable location. But the Hospitallers' task was to defend the city, and defense meant being where an attack would arrive, that is, along the landward walls. Enemies did not attack port cities from the sea because they couldn't undermine towers or transport battering rams by row boat!

What was strategically sound for the Grand Master of the Hospitaller Knights in the 12th century has proved equally valid for every ruler since. Over the years, every leader of Akko has taken advantage of this well-protected spot by building fortresses and governors' houses and prisons on top of the castle. Even the notorious Akko Prison—site of the most famous prison break in the country's history (involving 255 prisoners and memorialized in the film *Exodus*)—was built right on top of the Crusader castle. Now a memorial, the prison held common criminals as well as Jewish resistance fighters jailed for antigovernment activity during the British Mandate. Visitors can view a video presentation and model of the prison break, the gallows in the ghastly death-row chamber (where condemned prisoners were hanged) and a new memorial room.

Most impressive of all, the castle room is a great vaulted Gothic hall, which has been identified as the dining hall of the Hospitaller knights. A *fleur-de-lis* graces the corner of the groin vault (the Hospitallers were mostly French), and the room itself is the best example of Gothic architecture in the country. It also leads us to the underground of the underground: a network of tunnels dug beneath the now-buried Crusader buildings. To protect themselves from hostile neighbors, the Hospitallers constructed underground tunnels that led from one end of their quarter to the other and from their castle to their hospital.

The tunnel through the underground city opens onto a restored covered market street, where local artists and craftsmen have been encouraged to open stalls.

From the market, it's an easy stroll across the city to the seawall. The present Old City walls were built by the Muslims in the 18th and 19th centuries. For a wonderful, romantic view of the

ISRAEL MINISTRY OF TOURISM

Three of the seven Knights' Halls in the Hospitaller fortress in Akko can be visited today. The Hospitallers, or Knights of the Order of St. John, were founded
to care for ailing pilgrims, but the order soon became an elite fighting force.

walls along the sea and of Haifa and the Carmel Mountains in the far distance, I like to walk along the wall from the northernmost tower (Burj el-Kuraijim) to the lighthouse in the south. At the southern end is the most beautiful *khan* (caravansary), with alternating pillars of gray and Aswan-pink granite, I have ever seen. Once a way-station for caravans, the *khan* was built in 1785 by el-Jazzar.

By the time we reach the harbor, we have forgotten that this is Israel and half imagine ourselves on a Mediterranean island. Now, the pangs of hunger have taken over. What luck—a number of good restaurants are right here along the harbor. I think fondly of the night some years ago when 13 of us enjoyed dining here on one gigantic *lokus* (grouper) fish! A memorable evening indeed.

BIBLICAL ARCHAEOLOGY SOCIETY

Illuminating Archaeology and the Bible

The Biblical Archaeology Society, publisher of *Biblical Archaeology Review, Bible Review* and *Archaeology Odyssey*, was founded in 1974 as a nonprofit, nondenominational, educational organization dedicated to the dissemination of information about archaeology and the Bible.

Other books from Biblical Archaeology Society include:

Ancient Israel:
*From Abraham to the Roman
Destruction of the Temple*

Christianity and Rabbinic Judaism:
*A Parallel History of their
Origins and Early Development*

Mysteries of the Bible:
*From the Garden of Eden to
the Shroud of Turin*

Abraham & Family:
*New Insights into the
Patriarchal Narratives*

For more information about these and other products from Biblical Archaeology Society, including DVDs, CD-ROMs and videos, please visit **www.biblicalarchaeology.org/store**.